Dogmatism

Dogmatism

Dogmatism

On the History of a Scholarly Vice

**HERMAN PAUL AND
ALEXANDER STOEGER**

BLOOMSBURY ACADEMIC
LONDON • NEW YORK • OXFORD • NEW DELHI • SYDNEY

BLOOMSBURY ACADEMIC
Bloomsbury Publishing Plc
50 Bedford Square, London, WC1B 3DP, UK
1385 Broadway, New York, NY 10018, USA
29 Earlsfort Terrace, Dublin 2, Ireland

BLOOMSBURY, BLOOMSBURY ACADEMIC and the Diana logo are trademarks of
Bloomsbury Publishing Plc

First published in Great Britain 2024

Cover image: *Where Heaven and Earth Meet*, 1888
Science History Images/Alamy Stock Photo

Bloomsbury Publishing Plc does not have any control over, or responsibility for, any third-
party websites referred to or in this book. All internet addresses given in this book were
correct at the time of going to press. The author and publisher regret any inconvenience
caused if addresses have changed or sites have ceased to exist, but can accept no
responsibility for any such changes.

A catalogue record for this book is available from the British Library.

A catalog record for this book is available from the Library of Congress.

ISBN: HB: 978-1-3503-8264-0
PB: 978-1-3503-8263-3
ePDF: 978-1-3503-9957-0
eBook: 978-1-3503-9955-6

Typeset by Deanta Global Publishing Services, Chennai, India
Printed and bound in Great Britain

To find out more about our authors and books visit www.bloomsbury.com and sign up for
our newsletters.

Contents

Acknowledgments

This short book emerges out of the research project "Scholarly Vices: A Longue Durée History" led by Herman Paul at Leiden University. We would like to thank all project members (Edurne De Wilde, Kim Hajek, Anne Por, Hidde Slotboom, Sjang ten Hagen) for valuable conversations and helpful feedback over the years. We owe a special word of thanks to Caroline Schep, the project's research assistant from 2020 to 2022, who helped us enormously with preliminary research for several chapters of the book. Her successor, Marieke Nolten, carefully prepared the index. We thank the audiences who listened and responded to our work in progress in a PCNI seminar organized by Dario Fazzi at Leiden University (May 2022) and a panel at the tenth annual conference of the Society for the History of the Humanities (November 2022), where Ian James Kidd provided stimulating commentary. Also, we are indebted to the anonymous reviewers for their comments and suggestions. It is a pleasure once again to thank Emily Drewe, Megan Harris, and their colleagues at Bloomsbury for a smooth and pleasant cooperation. Both our research and the open-access publication of this title were funded by a Vici grant from the Dutch Research Council (NWO).

1

Introduction

Why do molecular biologists so often resemble Greg Lestrade, the well-meaning but naive Scotland Yard inspector known to all readers of Sherlock Holmes detective stories? Medical oncologist Prakash Kulkarni raised this question in a 2021 article on "the perils of dogmatism in science" to criticize his colleagues for being insufficiently committed to exploring untrodden research paths. Although many of them must have read enough Sherlock Holmes stories to know that the genius of Arthur Conan Doyle's detective consists in taking seriously what others put aside as irrelevant information, they seem to follow in Lestrade's footsteps rather than in Holmes'. Like Lestrade, they look for obvious clues, from which they draw seemingly convincing conclusions without "recognizing, much less considering, alternative and plausible explanations." For Kulkarni, this lack of open-mindedness, so characteristically unlike Holmes, was most evident in his colleagues' "dogmatic" adherence to a theory proposed in the early 1950s by Francis Crick. According to this theory, information passed from nucleic acids (DNA or RNA) into proteins cannot be transferred back. While this may be true in a great many cases, Kulkarni argued that it is "dogmatic" or closed-minded to believe a priori that it applies to each and every protein. Instead of asserting "dogmatically that [Crick's theory] is correct," biologists should consider the possibility that some proteins behave differently. Dogmatic thinking, in other words, hinders progress in science, just as it fails to solve the murder case in Doyle's detective story, "The Boscombe Valley Mystery."[1]

Although Inspector Lestrade does not appear frequently in scientific papers, Kulkarni's outburst against dogmatism is quite typical. Countless are the occasions on which scientists warn their students against dogmatism,

---

[1] Prakash Kulkarni, "The Boscombe Valley Mystery: A Lesson in the Perils of Dogmatism in Science," *Journal of Biosciences* 46 (2021): 59:1–9, at 2.

accuse their opponents of dogmatic reasoning, or pride themselves on having moved beyond the dogmatism of a previous generation. The vice is known across the academic spectrum, from paleontologists and biologists such as Stephen Jay Gould ("absence of dogmatism is the truest mark of a great scientist") to literary scholars like Wayne C. Booth (who wrote an angry book against the "modern dogma" that one has understood a literary text once the author's secret motive has been identified).[2] Charges of dogmatism are found in student textbooks, in book reviews ("the glaciological discussions contain long sequences of dogmatic statements"), as well as in moments of controversy ("sociobiology makes the most dogmatic assertions").[3] And although dogmatism may take on different roles across this range of fields and genres, it almost always has an accusatory ring to it. The term typically refers to what philosophers call an "epistemic vice": a trait of character that hampers the pursuit of epistemic aims such as knowledge and understanding of the world.[4]

Nothing of this is new. Ever since Antiquity, scholars have assigned the label "dogmatists" to colleagues with whom they disagreed.[5] Originating in Greek philosophy (not in Christian theology, as many seem to think), the term initially did not have pejorative connotations. It only acquired them in the early modern period, when scholars in and around the Royal Society came to regard experimental science as a remedy to "the vanity of dogmatizing." If this turned dogmatism into a scholarly vice, eighteenth-century authors added another layer of meaning: they equated dogmatism with believing on authority. As this squared badly with Enlightenment ideals of thinking for oneself ("sapere aude"), dogmatic thinking was increasingly portrayed as old-fashioned or as an obstacle to progress.[6] Both elements

---

[2] Stephen Jay Gould, "Prologue," in Gould, *Hen's Teeth and Horse's Toes: Further Reflections in Natural History* (New York: W. W. Norton, 1983), 11–16, at 16; Wayne C. Booth, *Modern Dogma and the Rhetoric of Assent* (Chicago: University of Chicago Press, 1974).

[3] Charles R. Bentley, review of *The Last Great Ice Sheets* by George H. Denton and Terence J. Hughes, *Science* 213, no. 4509 (1981): 752–3, at 753; James P. Hurd, *Investigating the Biological Foundations of Human Morality* (Lewiston: Edwin Mellen, 1996), 132.

[4] Quassim Cassam, *Vices of the Mind: From the Intellectual to the Political* (Oxford: Oxford University Press, 2019); Alessandra Tanesini, *The Mismeasurement of the Self: A Study in Vice Epistemology* (Oxford: Oxford University Press, 2021); Ian James Kidd, Heather Battaly, and Quassim Cassam (eds.), *Vice Epistemology* (New York: Routledge 2021).

[5] See, for example, Dirk C. Baltzly, "Who Are the Mysterious Dogmatists of *Adversus Mathematicus* ix 352?" *Ancient Philosophy* 18 (1998): 145–70—yet another article that invokes the inspiration of Sherlock Holmes: "If we may liken the search for the identity of 'The Dogmatists' in the passage from Sextus to a murder mystery, I think that all the philological evidence establishes is that the Stoics are suspects."

[6] As a preliminary study for this project has argued for the *Geisteswissenschaften* in nineteenth-century Germany: Caroline Schep and Herman Paul, "Denial of Coevalness: Charges of Dogmatism in the Nineteenth-Century Humanities," *History of European Ideas* 48, no. 6 (2022): 778–94.

came to good use when scholars in the nineteenth century had to justify the aims and methods of their newly created academic disciplines. The trope of dogmatism allowed them to fashion themselves as scientific avant-gardes whose commitment to "critical" analysis and "objective" research sharply contrasted with the "uncritical" and "dogmatic" beliefs of earlier generations. The rest, one might say, is history: Booth, Gould, Kulkarni, *e tutti quanti* drew on this legacy.

* * *

Why does this history merit our attention? There are three answers to the question. The first is that modern charges of dogmatism are unintelligible without a knowledge of the history behind them. In some cases, this reliance on earlier uses of the term is pretty obvious. When environmental economist Herman E. Daly lashed out against "the unison snoring of supine economists in deep dogmatic slumber" (because they failed to recognize that economic growth cannot continue indefinitely), he almost literally quoted Immanuel Kant's statement, more than two centuries earlier, that David Hume had awakened him from his "dogmatic slumber."[7] If historical knowledge in this case helps one grasp the allusion, it is even more relevant in cases when scientists seem unaware of the historical baggage attached to the term. Only a broad familiarity with the different meanings and functions that dogmatism has historically acquired allows one to recognize that, for instance, Gould and Booth used the same word to refer to different things. Dogmatism for Gould was the opposite of open-mindedness, a virtue that he saw embodied by Charles Darwin (insofar as Darwin was no stubborn defender of his theory but someone welcoming questions and objections). For Booth, by contrast, dogmas were unexamined habits or ideas that had become fashionable even though they could not stand up to critical scrutiny.[8] It is easier to recognize these distinct uses of the term if one has some knowledge of the concept's rich and varied history.

Historical knowledge is even more crucial for understanding the Crick "dogma" that Prakash Kulkarni referred to in our opening example. In a famous 1957 lecture, Crick argued that information passed into protein cannot get out again. To the confusion of many, he called this hypothesis the

---

[7] Herman E. Daly, *Beyond Growth: The Economics of Sustainable Development* (Boston: Beacon Press, 1996), 145. Similarly: Herman E. Daly, *From Uneconomic Growth to a Steady-State Economy* (Cheltenham: Edward Elgar, 2014), 16.

[8] Gould, "Prologue," 16; Booth, *Modern Dogma*, 25.

"central dogma" of molecular biology.[9] Clearly, this phrase was not aimed at discrediting his own hypothesis. On the contrary, for Crick, a central dogma was something like a general principle: a broad-ranging hypothesis that was not yet definitively confirmed but plausible in light of ongoing research on DNA and RNA. Although Crick would later say that his use of the term "dogma" had been confusing,[10] it actually followed established usage. Before "dogmatic" became a vice, the adjective referred to a systematic mode of ordering scholarly knowledge (as distinguished from a historical or empirical mode focused on how knowledge is acquired).[11] From a historical perspective, therefore, Crick's seemingly confusing or idiosyncratic terminology turns out to make perfect sense.

What these examples illustrate is a need for subjecting such a well-known, often-used, and often ill-defined term as "dogmatism" to historical scrutiny. We need a history that traces what scholars understood "dogmatism" to mean, why they invoked the term in the most diverse of contexts, and how their usages show both continuity and discontinuity over time. This is the first objective of this book: it seeks to make current talk of dogmatism intelligible by pointing out how it relies on or deviates from patterns of meaning and usage established over the course of centuries.

*   *   *

Related to this first objective is a second reason for subjecting scholars' talk of dogmatism to historical scrutiny. To the extent that warnings against the ills of dogmatism drew, and still draw, on established meanings and uses of the term, they allow us to make a methodological contribution to the historiography of scholarly virtues and vices. In the past two decades, scholarly virtues and vices—that is, the habits of mind that scholars are expected to display and to avoid, respectively—have become a serious topic of research. New books, journal articles, and conference papers appear on an annual basis, sometimes written by philosophers but increasingly also by historians. Historical research, however, can take on different forms, depending on the questions scholars

---

[9] F. H. C. Crick, "On Protein Synthesis," *Symposia of the Society for Experimental Biology* 12 (1958): 138–63, at 152.
[10] Horace Freeland Judson, *The Eighth Day of Creation: Makers of the Revolution in Biology* (New York: Simon and Schuster, 1979), 337; Francis Crick, *What Mad Pursuit: A Personal View of Scientific Discovery* (London: Penguin, 1990), 109.
[11] More on this in Chapter 2.

ask, the methods they use, and the sources on which they rely. This prompts the question: How can the history of virtues or vices best be written?[12]

So far, two approaches have been dominant. First, there is a *universalizing* approach, represented by the German philosopher Jürgen Habermas. Acknowledging that philosophers' vocabularies change over time, Habermas notes that the *term* "dogmatism" as defined by Immanuel Kant did not exist prior to the 1780s. This, however, does not imply that the *concept* was unknown to earlier generations of philosophers. According to Habermas, French encyclopedists like Baron d'Holbach were well acquainted with the dangers of dogmatism, even though they called the vice by other names, such as "prejudice." Similarly, Habermas argues that ideologies and philosophies of history of the sort that Karl Popper in the 1940s condemned as "historicism" can all be classified under the rubric of dogmatism. From this perspective, Plato already was a dogmatist, not because ancient Greek opponents charged him with this vice, but because he meets Habermas' own Kantian-inspired definition of dogmatism. This approach is *universalizing* insofar as it operates with timeless categories of vice, construed in such a way as to transcend the contingencies of philosophers' language. Consequently, it offers little historical insight, except that vices can be described in different idioms.[13]

Historians have responded to this deficiency by developing alternative lines of inquiry. Inspired by Lorraine Daston and Peter Galison's *Objectivity*,[14] some have traced the histories of individual virtues like impartiality, sympathy, empathy, and magnanimity.[15] Others have reconstructed catalogs of virtues and vices at specific moments in time—the "vices of the learned" as defined in neo-Latin treatises, for instance—or examined more generally why imitating exemplars of virtue was so important to early modern men of

---

[12] On which, see also Herman Paul, "An Ethos of Criticism: Virtues and Vices in Nineteenth-Century Strasbourg," in Herman Paul (ed.), *Writing the History of the Humanities: Questions, Themes, and Approaches* (London: Bloomsbury, 2023), 193–216.

[13] Jürgen Habermas, "Dogmatismus, Vernunft und Entscheidung: Zu Theorie und Praxis in der verwissenschaftliche Zivilisation," in Habermas, *Theorie und Praxis: Sozialphilosophische Studien* (Neuwied am Rhein: Luchterhand, 1963), 231–57, at 234, 241 n. 2. For Popper's understanding of historicism, see *The Poverty of Historicism* (London: Routledge and Kegan Paul, 1957).

[14] Lorraine Daston and Peter Galison, *Objectivity* (New York: Zone Books, 2007). See also Lorraine Daston, "Objectivity and Impartiality: Epistemic Virtues in the Humanities," in Rens Bod, Jaap Maat, and Thijs Weststeijn (eds.), *The Making of the Humanities*, vol. 3 (Amsterdam: Amsterdam University Press, 2014), 27–41.

[15] Kathryn Murphy and Anita Traninger (eds.), *The Emergence of Impartiality* (Leiden: Brill, 2014); Eric Schliesser (ed.), *Sympathy: A History* (Oxford: Oxford University Press, 2015); Susan Lanzioni, *Empathy: A History* (New Haven: Yale University Press, 2018); Sophia Vasalou (ed.), *The Measure of Greatness: Philosophers on Magnanimity* (Oxford: Oxford University Press, 2019).

learning.[16] What is most characteristic of this scholarship is its interest in what people understood empathy, impartiality, or objectivity to mean. It carefully distinguishes between different meanings that different authors attributed to the same term, while also disentangling medical, theological, and philosophical strands of thinking about the nature of vice.[17] So, whereas the Habermasean approach is *universalizing*, historical scholarship is often *particularizing*. From this follows a second difference. While the first approach transcends the contingencies of history by focusing on a well-delineated *concept* (dogmatism as defined by Habermas), the latter's interest in historical particularities goes hand in hand with great attentiveness to the *terminology* used by historical actors. Consequently, whereas dogmatism serves as an analytical category in the first approach, it appears as an actor's category in the second one.

In line with the first objective of this book—making intelligible what people mean when they talk about dogmatism—our sympathies lie with the latter approach more than with the former. The story told in this book is not about dogmatism as defined by modern philosophical authorities. Neither is it a history of scientists, approaches, and arguments that we regard as dogmatic, or an account of how dogmatic scientific stances have accompanied and competed with more empirical stances.[18] Instead, this is a book about "dogmatism" as a vice term invoked by scholars in the most diverse of contexts. It is a history of how scholars across the centuries thought, wrote, and quarreled about dogmatism, how they accused each other of dogmatic conduct or arguments, and how the meanings and connotations of this actor's category evolved over time. Accordingly, this book is methodologically indebted to *Begriffsgeschichte* (conceptual history)—a branch of intellectual history highly sensitive to how concepts, idioms, or vocabularies develop over time, what they do and do not allow people to say, and what they reveal about the social, political, or religious contexts in which they are invoked.[19]

---

[16] Sari Kivistö, *The Vices of Learning: Morality and Knowledge at Early Modern Universities* (Leiden: Brill, 2014); Sorana Corneanu, *Regimens of the Mind: Boyle, Locke, and the Early Modern Cultura Animi Tradition* (Chicago: University of Chicago Press, 2011); Hilaire Kallendorf, *Ambiguous Antidotes: Virtue as Vaccine for Vice in Early Modern Spain* (Toronto: University of Toronto Press, 2017).

[17] On the latter, see Ian James Kidd, "Deep Epistemic Vices," *Journal of Philosophical Research* 43 (2018): 43–67.

[18] Our phrasing here alludes to Bas C. van Fraassen, *The Empirical Stance* (New Haven: Yale University Press, 2002).

[19] Ernst Müller and Falko Schmieder, *Begriffsgeschichte zur Einführung* (Hamburg: Junius, 2020); Mark Bevir and Hans Erich Bödeker (eds.), *Begriffsgeschichte, Diskursgeschichte, Metapherngeschichte* (Göttingen: Wallstein, 2002); Melvin Richter, *The History of Political and Social Concepts: A Critical Introduction* (Oxford: Oxford University Press, 1995).

In one crucial respect, however, our study distinguishes itself from *Begriffsgeschichte* as conventionally practiced. While conceptual historians are often particularly interested in mapping changing *meanings* of terms, this book offers more than a history of meanings. What is noteworthy about Crick, Daly, Gould, and Booth is not merely that they *defined* dogmatism differently but also that they *harked back* to older, sometimes even centuries-old uses of the term. For this reason, a focus on changing meanings is important but not sufficient: it would leave out the *repertoires* on which authors drew in making their cases for or against dogmatism. We understand such repertoires to include conventional arguments, proverbial expressions ("dogmatic slumber"), classic dichotomies (dogmatism vs. criticism), oft-repeated arguments, and established ways of reasoning. What these repertoires had in common is that they offered ready-made arguments and figures of speech that authors could adjust and apply to their own situations.[20] While their classic status made them easily recognizable, repertoires could also serve as sources of justification insofar as they allowed authors to "anchor" their arguments in the authority of someone like Kant.[21]

Our second reason for undertaking a history of dogmatism is to make a case for the methodological significance of these repertoires and anchoring practices. As dogmatism "has a long history entangled with all sorts of epistemological, theological, and scientific issues,"[22] it lends itself well to illustrating a "third way" between the universalizing and particularizing approaches mentioned earlier. A history attentive to how critics of dogmatism explicitly or implicitly drew on old repertoires allows us to identify continuities over time that would remain invisible with an approach focused solely on changing meanings. These continuities, however, are no philosophical universals but historically contingent patterns created by authors who echoed, quoted, or otherwise alluded to earlier stages in the history of dogmatism. Methodologically, this points to a promising middle course between universalizing and particularizing modes of interpretation. What distinguishes our approach from particularizing modes of reading is that it draws sustained attention to the persistence of old habits, the reuse of time-honored arguments, and the explicit or implicit invocation of ancient authorities. The continuities over time that this approach brings to light are, however, unlike those of the universalizing approach

[20] See Ann Swidler, *Talk of Love: How Culture Matters* (Chicago: University of Chicago Press, 2001) and Paul McLean, *The Art of the Network: Strategic Interaction and Patronage in Renaissance Florence* (Durham: Duke University Press, 2007), 1–34.

[21] Ineke Sluiter, "Anchoring Innovation: A Classical Research Agenda," *European Review* 25, no. 1 (2017): 20–38.

[22] Ian James Kidd, "A Case for a Historical Vice Epistemology," *Humana Mente* 14, no. 39 (2021): 69–86, at 78.

exemplified by Habermas. They are no timeless universals but contingent products of rhetorical practices pursued in specific historical contexts.

*   *   *

Our third and final reason for tracing scholars' talk of dogmatism over time follows from the previous ones. Most philosophical literature on epistemic virtues and vices treats dogmatism as a character trait or an ingrained habit of thinking that prevents individuals from achieving epistemic success.[23] At first sight, this is an uncontroversial assumption: many of the scholars featured in this book (though not all of them) would have agreed with it. However, if we examine on what occasions and for what purposes these authors invoked the vice of dogmatism, it turns out that the issues at stake were often much larger than individuals' dispositional inability to acquire epistemic goals. Dogmatism was invoked most notably in large-scale border conflicts between science on the one hand and religion or politics on the other. Never was the term used with greater intensity than in nineteenth-century controversies over biblical criticism (Chapter 3) and Darwinian biology (Chapter 4), among American psychologists in Cold War America (Chapter 7), and in the evolution-creationism controversies of the 1970s and 1980s (Chapter 8)—not to mention the Science Wars of the 1990s.[24] The most important issue in these cases was not whether some individual was guilty of dogmatism but, more broadly, how the pursuit of academic research related to Christian doctrine, anti-communist politics, or the education of the youth.

The case of dogmatism hence allows us to see that practices of "vice-charging" could serve purposes well beyond the disqualification of poorly talented individuals.[25] In many cases, the word "dogmatism" was used to convey that the integrity of scholarly research as such was at risk due to interference from outside. This is to say that the vice term was put into the service of what sociologist Thomas Gieryn calls "boundary work" between science and non-science, especially at moments when threats of

---

[23] For example, Robert C. Roberts and W. Jay Wood, *Intellectual Virtues: An Essay in Regulative Epistemology* (Oxford: Clarendon Press, 2007), 194–8; Heather Battaly, "Closed-Mindedness and Dogmatism," *Episteme* 15, no. 3 (2018): 261–82; Battaly, "Closed-Mindedness as an Intellectual Vice," in Christoph Kelp and John Greco (eds.), *Virtue Theoretic Epistemology: New Methods and Approaches* (Cambridge: Cambridge University Press, 2020), 15–41; Cassam, *Vices of the Mind*, 100–20.

[24] On which, see Keith Parsons (ed.), *The Science Wars: Debating Scientific Knowledge and Technology* (Amherst: Prometheus, 2003).

[25] "Vice charging" is a term borrowed from Ian James Kidd, "Charging Others with Epistemic Vice," *The Monist* 99, no. 2 (2016): 181–97.

"epistemic corruption" were seen as looming on the horizon.[26] Although we will encounter various strategies of boundary work—relegating opponents to a pre-scientific past (Chapter 3) or comparing them to infallible religious authorities (Chapter 4)—common to all of them was an attempt at guarding, challenging, or redrawing the borders between academic research and other societal pursuits. A history of dogmatism, therefore, is worth pursuing also for its potential to broaden the discussion from individuals' character vices to the integrity of scholarly research and the threats surrounding it.

* * *

This short book—one of a series of historical investigations carried out in the research project "Scholarly Vices: A Longue Durée History"—is guided by a simple question: How and why was dogmatism invoked by scholars and their critics in the past few centuries? That is, what meanings did it have and what purposes did it serve? We try to answer this question by studying the history of dogmatism along three analytical axes. We begin by tracing the *meanings* that scholars attached to dogmatism. What ills, if any, did the term refer to and why did authors deem it important to warn their readers against them?[27] In addition, we examine the *functions* that the term fulfilled. Was it a means for scientific boundary work, a rhetorical tool for scholarly self-fashioning, or an umbrella category for everything that scholars perceived as impeding scientific progress? Third, we try to understand the *repertoires* on which authors drew. What were the models they followed, the notions they relied upon, or the old meanings into which they breathed new life?

The sources on which we base our analysis include a broad range of "metascientific" texts, such as state-of-the-art surveys, commentaries on academic trends, histories of science, and obituaries. In addition, we examine book reviews as well as scholarly controversies (not seldom prompted by critical reviews). Although many of these texts have been identified with electronic search engines—this book could not have been written without Google Books, JSTOR, the Internet Archive, and the HathiTrust Digital

---

[26] Thomas F. Gieryn, "Boundary-Work and the Demarcation of Science from Non-Science: Strains and Interests in Professional Ideologies of Scientists," *American Sociological Review* 48, no. 6 (1983): 781–95; Ian James Kidd, "Epistemic Corruption and Social Oppression," in Ian James Kidd, Quassim Cassam, and Heather Battaly (eds.), *Vice Epistemology* (London: Routledge, 2020), 69–87.
[27] "Meanings" here amount to what Mark Bevir calls "hermeneutic meanings," or the meanings that historians try to find in pursuing the question: "What did an author mean when he said such and such?" Mark Bevir, *The Logic of the History of Ideas* (Cambridge: Cambridge University Press, 1999), 37–8.

Library[28]—all of these sources have been subjected to close reading. In our attempt to understand the concerns of authors writing at particular places and moments in time, we have made ample use of secondary literature. (Unfortunately, we are able to mention only a fraction of this scholarship in our footnotes, due to limitations of space and a reluctance to economize on primary source references.)

The book is arranged around a series of case studies, drawn from across the sciences, social sciences, and humanities. Although these are representative case studies in the sense of illustrating broader trends, the story told in this book is anything but comprehensive. As "dogmatism" was a word used in the most diverse of intellectual, cultural, and political contexts, there is no end to the case studies that could have been discussed in the chapters that follow. This is especially true if we take into account languages other than German, French, and English. As this book is almost entirely based on European and North American sources, there is ample room for follow-up studies on dogmatism in Asia or Africa. It is likely that a broader geographical scope will add different story elements and a greater variety of subplots. Nonetheless, the *capita selecta* explored in this book (in the spirit of David Armitage's "serial contextualism") are sufficiently diverse to illustrate both the semantic flexibility of the term and the variety of uses to which "dogmatism" could be put.[29] For the nineteenth and early twentieth centuries, we focus mainly on Europe, with lots of German, English, and French examples, but also some Italian and Spanish voices. In line with changing scientific power relations after the Second World War, American examples figure more prominently in the last two chapters. By the time we reach the early twenty-first century, in the second half of Chapter 8, geographical borders become blurred, as science is nowadays a rather global enterprise.

Given that we consistently treat dogmatism as an actor's category, it is worth noting that "scholars" is a term of our own, used to refer to researchers across the academic spectrum, from life scientists and natural scientists to social scientists and humanists. (Although the English word "scientist," coined in the 1830s, initially had a scope comparable to the German *Wissenschaftler*

---

[28] We started with simple keyword searches ("dogma," "dogmatic," and "dogmatism" in English, German, and French, occasionally also in other languages). In a second round, we added more specific search terms like "Hartmann," "Darwin," and "Rokeach." Although this returned many relevant hits, there are limits to what search engines can do. It is worth adding, therefore, that we found many relevant sources only by reading through an author's oeuvre or by browsing the volumes of a journal.

[29] David Armitage, "What's the Big Idea? Intellectual History and the Longue Durée," *History of European Ideas* 38, no. 4 (2012): 493–507.

and the Dutch *wetenschapper*, this is no longer the case.)[30] Similarly, we speak about "scholarly vices" instead of "epistemic vices" to convey that dogmatism was seen as undesirable, not merely because it was believed to have negative epistemic implications but also because, more often than not, there were religious or political issues at stake. Scholarly vices thus include habits of mind that scholars were supposed to avoid on other than merely epistemic grounds.[31]

* * *

Finally, a brief overview of the book might be in order. Chapter 2 traces the history of "dogmatism" from its earliest beginnings up until the late eighteenth century, when Immanuel Kant set his stamp on the term, not merely by drawing sharp contrasts between critical and dogmatic philosophy but also by depicting the latter as a relic from the past. Focusing on nineteenth-century narratives of scientific progress, Chapter 3 shows how dominant this connotation of obsoleteness became, also in controversies in which scholars accused of dogmatism effectively found themselves denied a legitimate place in the present. A second dominant connotation is discussed in Chapter 4, devoted to what James Moore calls the "post-Darwinian controversies" in late nineteenth-century Britain.[32] By accusing Darwin's critics of church-like dogmatism, Thomas Huxley and others imbued dogmatism with connotations of ecclesial authority—which in the wake of the Vatican Council was just as deadly an accusation as the charge of impeding scientific progress. Against this twofold background, Chapter 5 features some high-profile scholars that were turned into proverbial epitomes of dogmatism, just as some countries (Germany) and ethnic groups (Jews) were believed to have a greater inclination toward dogmatism than others.

If most of the authors discussed so far used dogmatism dismissively, as corresponding to a scholarly vice, Chapter 6 explores an alternative tradition in which dogmatism was understood as a necessary element or even a desirable goal of scientific inquiry. Warnings against dogmatism reappear in Chapter 7,

---

[30] Horst Grundlach, *Wissenschaftler: Vierhundert Jahre Begriffsgeschichte einer Wörtersippe* (Heidelberg: Winter, 2022); Denise Philipps, "Francis Bacon and the Germans: Stories From When 'Science' Meant '*Wissenschaft*,'" *History of Science* 53, no. 4 (2015): 378–94; Sydney Ross, "Scientist: The Story of a Word," *Annals of Science* 18, no. 2 (1962): 65–85.

[31] As argued at greater length in Christiaan Engberts and Herman Paul, "Scholarly Vices: Boundary Work in Nineteenth-Century Orientalism," in Jeroen van Dongen and Herman Paul (eds.), *Epistemic Virtues in the Sciences and the Humanities* (Cham: Springer, 2017), 79–90.

[32] James R. Moore, *The Post-Darwinian Controversies: A Study of the Protestant Struggle to Come to Terms with Darwin in Great Britain and America, 1870–1900* (Cambridge: Cambridge University Press, 1979).

but in a different guise than before, as psychologists in Cold War America developed a "dogmatism scale" to measure dogmatic thinking habits with quasi-scientific precision. Instead of accusing one another of dogmatism, the scholars examined in this chapter studied dogmatism with the aim of promoting open-mindedness as a civic and political virtue. Chapter 8, finally, argues that dogmatism in the second half of the twentieth century transformed from a character vice into a theory vice—that is, into a feature not of persons but of theories. But even as dogmatism in the classic sense of an undesirable character trait lost ground to dogmas understood as well-entrenched beliefs hampering the progress of science, older and newer voices alike continued to warn students against the vice of closed-mindedness, thereby keeping an old tradition alive. In the conclusion (Chapter 9), we bring these threads together and offer some tentative reflections on how dogmatism compares to other scholarly virtues and vices.

2

Origins of the Term
Ancient Layers of Meaning

Where does the term "dogmatism" come from? When Rudolf Eisler, a Jewish private scholar in fin-de-siècle Vienna, stumbled upon this question in compiling a dictionary of philosophical concepts, he discovered that the question allowed for two answers. On the one hand, *Dogmatismus* had strong Kantian connotations. In a philosophical climate dominated by the legacy of Kantian Idealism, charges of dogmatism almost instantly evoked the authority of Immanuel Kant, who in his *Critique of Pure Reason* (1781) had denounced dogmatism as the uncritical habit of accepting philosophical beliefs without examining whether these beliefs are epistemologically justified. On the other hand, Eisler was sufficiently versed in the history of philosophy to know that "dogmatism," "dogmatic," and "dogmatists" were terms with long pedigrees. Already in the first centuries CE, Diogenes Laërtius and others had distinguished between "skeptics" (σκεπτικοί) and "dogmatists" (δογματικοί).[1] Drawing on such ancient typologies, early modern thinkers like Blaise Pascal had also wrestled with the philosophical extremes of "dogmatism" and "Pyrrhonism" (named after Pyrrho, the skeptic philosopher), neither of which Pascal found particularly attractive.[2] Eisler thus saw himself confronted with two genealogies: a short-term history of dogmatism that started with Kant and a long-term narrative that reached much further back in time.

---

[1] Diogenes Laërtius, *Lives of Eminent Philosophers*, trans. R. D. Hicks, vol. 2 (London: William Heinemann, 1925), 487, 491 (IX.74, 77).
[2] Blaise Pascal, "Pensées," in Pascal, *Pensées and Other Writings*, trans. Honor Levi, ed. Anthony Levi (Oxford: Oxford University Press, 1995), 1–181, at 9, 11, 41–2.

Judging by the first and second editions of his *Dictionary of Philosophical Concepts and Expressions* (1899, 1904), Eisler was not sure how to reconcile these stories of origins. In the first edition, he highlighted the continuities between Diogenes, Pascal, and Kant by discussing all of them under the single heading of *Dogmatismus* (adding, however, that "the new meaning of dogmatism stems from KANT").[3] In the second edition, however, Eisler emphasized Kant's distinctiveness by moving all pre-1781 material to a separate entry. This allowed him to present "dogmatism," with the pejorative "ism," as a term originating in Kant. Insofar as Eisler in this second edition drew attention to different uses of the term, he limited himself to post-Kantian philosophers like Johann Gottlieb Fichte, Georg Wilhelm Friedrich Hegel, and Eduard von Hartmann.[4] By 1904, therefore, it seemed as if pre-Kantian occurrences of dogmatism could be relegated to the past. They had existed but hardly mattered anymore in a world where no one wanted, or believed it to be possible, to go back before Kant.

One wonders: How convincing is this thesis? Is it, more than a century after Eisler, still plausible to maintain that Kant marked a watershed in the history of dogmatism? Did Eisler see correctly that discontinuity in meaning (Kant giving new twists to an existing term) outweighed continuity in vocabulary (Kant not being the first to use the adjective "dogmatic")? If we find nineteenth- or twentieth-century academics accusing one another of dogmatism, can we say that they did so in the wake of Kant's *Critique of Pure Reason*?

By and large, recent scholarship tends to answer this question affirmatively.[5] Even Hubert Filser, a German historian of theology who spends more than 800 pages analyzing what "dogma" and "dogmatics" meant in early modern Europe, agrees that it was Kant who gave dogmatism its characteristically modern shape. Without mentioning Eisler by name, Filser accepts his thesis that the term has been used post-1781 largely within Kantian parameters— that is, as denoting an essentially uncritical, epistemologically unreflective mode of thinking. According to Filser, this is partly because most nineteenth- and twentieth-century authors used "dogmatism" as a term of abuse, not descriptively but polemically, just as Kant had done in denouncing Gottfried Wilhelm Leibniz, Christian Wolff, and others as epistemologically naïve dogmatists. More importantly, the polemical "ism" was a Kantian invention. While "dogma" and "dogmatic" were terms widely used in early

---

[3] Rudolf Eisler, *Wörterbuch der philosophischen Begriffe und Ausdrücke* (Berlin: Ernst Siegfried Mittler und Sohn, 1899), 171.
[4] Rudolf Eisler, *Wörterbuch der philosophischen Begriffe*, 2nd ed., vol. 1 (Berlin: Ernst Siegfried Mittler und Sohn, 1904), 230–1.
[5] See, for example, W. Nieke, "Dogmatismus," in Joachim Ritter (ed.), *Historisches Wörterbuch der Philosophie*, vol. 2 (Darmstadt: Wissenschaftliche Buchgesellschaft, 1972), 277–9.

modern Europe, "dogmatism" gained traction only after 1781.[6] If anything, this suggests that Kant's significance for the story of this book is hard to overestimate.

This chapter will argue, nonetheless, that the origins of dogmatism are more multi-faceted than accounts like Eisler's convey. Drawing on the excellent scholarship of Maximilian Herberger in particular,[7] we will argue, first of all, that at least two of the allegedly Kantian features of the term— the "ism" ending and its polemical pejorative use—had historical precedents in early modern Europe. Although we do not deny that Kant's interventions were hugely influential, the Königsberg philosopher relied more heavily on existing discourses than Eisler allowed his readers to see. A second reason for drawing attention to the pre-Kantian history of dogmatism is that this book covers a much broader area than the history of philosophy to which Eisler limited himself. This broader perspective brings into relief the limitations of successionist narratives like Eisler's (i.e., stories of Kant's "dogmatism" replacing earlier uses of the term). Even if philosophers in the Kantian tradition did not show much interest in pre-Kantian notions of dogmatic reasoning, scholars in other fields and other traditions more than once revived old layers of meanings.

* * *

When Eisler quoted Diogenes Laërtius as saying that ancient philosophy was divided into two camps, the σκεπτικοί and the δογματικοί, he hit perhaps unknowingly on something important. Diogenes' juxtaposition of skeptics and dogmatists was a characteristic move, typical of how the term "dogmatic" was used, not only in the first centuries CE but also long afterward. Dogmatic was part of a typology that Diogenes used to map different schools, methods, or approaches in Greek and Roman philosophy. While skeptics like Pyrrho were "constantly engaged in overthrowing the dogmas of all schools," dogmatists were those who looked upon this endless questioning with incomprehension, complaining that "the Sceptics do away with life itself, in that they reject all that life consists in." Although Diogenes hinted at the possibility of "dogmatic" also being used accusatorily, especially in stating that some dogmatists were eager to alert their skeptical opponents to the "dogmatizing" elements in their own reasoning, the most important function of the distinction between

---

[6] Hubert Filser, *Dogma, Dogmen, Dogmatik: Eine Untersuchung zur Begründung und zur Entstehungsgeschichte einer theologischen Disziplin von der Reformation bis zur Spätaufklärung* (Munster: LIT, 2001), 17 n. 32, 517.

[7] Maximilian Herberger, *Dogmatik: Zur Geschichte von Begriff und Methode in Medizin und Jurisprudenz* (Frankfurt am Main: Vittorio Klostermann, 1981).

skeptics and dogmatists was to classify philosophers into broadly recognizable groups.[8]

Although dogmatists were most frequently contrasted with skeptics or Pyrrhonists, other typologies from the early centuries CE also included "empiricists" or "academicians" (named after Plato's Ἀκαδημία). Sextus Empiricus, to mention but one example, argued that "the main types of philosophy are thought to be three in number: the Dogmatic, the Academic, and the Skeptic."[9] Most of these typologies were forgotten during the so-called Middle Ages.[10] They reentered philosophers' vocabulary, however, with the revival of ancient skepticism in the sixteenth century.[11] Montaigne's *Essays* (1580), for instance, relied heavily on Sextus in depicting the philosophical scene as one great battle between Doubters, Dogmatists, and Academicians:

> All philosophers may be divided into three schools: those who think they have discovered the truth; those who think it can not be discovered; those who are still looking for it. The Peripatetics, Epicureans, Stoics, and others—the Dogmatists, the Aristotelians—have believed it found; the Academicians and others have judged that it could not be attained by us; Pyrrho and other Sceptics have persisted in the search, using doubt for their instrument of investigation.[12]

Whereas later generations would argue that Plato together with Socrates had "laid the foundation of a metaphysical dogmatism,"[13] Montaigne seemed unsure how to classify Plato: "Some have thought Plato a Dogmatist, others a doubter, others, on certain subjects the former, on certain subjects the latter." Yet, even this example confirms that Montaigne saw ancient Greek philosophy as navigating between a cultivating of "doubt and ignorance" on the one hand, and a "hunting for truth," on the other.[14] Likewise, one of the most famous passages in Pascal's *Pensées* (1669), about the "glory and reject of the universe" that human beings are, appears in the context of a meditation on the perennial tension between Pyrrhonists (unable to prove that principles

---

[8] Diogenes, *Lives*, vol. 2, 487, 515, 513 (IX, 74, 104, 102).

[9] Sextus Empiricus, "Outlines of Pyrrhonism," in *The Skeptic Way: Sextus Empiricus's Outlines of Pyrrhonism*, trans. Benson Mates (Oxford: Oxford University Press, 1996), 87–217, at 89 (*Pyr.* I, 1).

[10] Herberger, *Dogmatik*, 171–2; Filser, *Dogma*, 62–4.

[11] On which, see Richard H. Popkin, *The History of Scepticism: From Savonarola to Bayle*, rev. ed. (Oxford: Oxford University Press, 2003), esp. 17–43.

[12] Montaigne, *Essays*, trans. George B. Ives and Grace Norton, vol. 2 (Cambridge, MA: Harvard University Press, 1925), 175. Cf. Sextus, "Outlines," 89 (*Pyr.* I, 1).

[13] Bolingbroke, *Fragments or Minutes of Essays* (London: David Mallet, 1754), 253.

[14] Montaigne, *Essays*, 275, 272.

of good and true are more than dreamlike illusions) and dogmatists (convinced that "we cannot doubt natural principles").[15]

Although none of these examples offer clear definitions of dogmatism, they do show that the adjective "dogmatic" emerged in tandem with other, contrastive terms. "Dogmatism" was not a stand-alone term but a typological concept that derived its meaning partly from the approaches (skepticism, Pyrrhonism) with which it was contrasted.

* * *

The adjective "dogmatic," nonetheless, always remained tied to its root, the noun "dogma." Accordingly, some knowledge of what δογμα meant in ancient Greece and Rome is crucial for understanding the connotations that "dogmatic" and "dogmatism" acquired. Without any claim to comprehensiveness, we would like to highlight two meanings, both of which would cast a long shadow over the history traced in this book.[16]

The first one can be found in Quintilian's *The Orator's Education* (*c.* 95 CE). Speaking about Plato's dialogues, the Roman rhetorician noticed that they were not all written for the same purpose: "Some of his dialogues were composed to refute opponents, and these are called 'elenctic' dialogues, while others are for teaching, and are called 'dogmatic.'"[17] Although it is unknown to what extent Quintilian was aware of the etymological affinity between *dogma* and *docere* (teaching), it is important that he portrayed Plato as someone transmitting δογματα to students.[18] Dogmata, for Quintilian, were the sort of beliefs that constituted an educational curriculum.

A second, more technical concept of dogma can be found in Galen, the Greek physician who in the second century CE tried to synthesize the "dogmatic," "empirical," and "methodical" medical schools of his day. The bone of contention between these schools was the relationship between theory and practice. Did medicine start with observations (taking the pulse of a patient) or with theories about the human body (such as Hippocrates' humoral theory)?[19] Although Galen followed conventional practice in using

---

[15] Pascal, "Pensées," 41.

[16] Detailed conceptual histories of the term can be found in Herberger, *Dogmatik*, and Filser, *Dogma*.

[17] Quintilian, *The Orator's Education, Books 1–2*, trans. Donald A. Russell (Cambridge, MA: Harvard University Press, 2001), 363 (*Inst.* II, 15, 26).

[18] Herberger, *Dogmatik*, 80.

[19] A succinct overview of ancient medical schools can be found in Danielle Gourevitch, "The Paths of Knowledge: Medicine in the Roman World," in Mirko D. Grmek (ed.), *Western Medical Thought from Antiquity to the Middle Ages*, trans. Antony Shugaar (Cambridge, MA: Harvard University Press, 1998), 104–38.

"dogmatists" as a descriptive label for anti-empiricist physicians,[20] he showed a special interest in dogmatists who relied on experience more than on theoretical knowledge as well as in empiricists who approached their patients like "semi-Dogmatics."[21] Following these dogmatic empiricists or empiricist dogmatists, Galen developed a notion of dogma that Herberger characterizes as a "middle road" between two extremes. For Galen, δογματα were universal statements about the causes or symptoms of an illness, produced by human reasoning but convincing only as long as they were supported by experience.[22]

Each in its own way, these two notions of δογμα would prove influential, not only in the late antique and medieval periods but also well into the early modern era. Galen's model, for instance, was foundational for the emergence of *medicina dogmatica* in the sixteenth century and the subsequent development of *theologia dogmatica* in the seventeenth century.[23] What distinguished dogmatic theology from historical theology was not its subject matter but its methodological priority of synthesis over analysis. While *historia* was understood to refer to individual matters of fact, dogmas were presented as generalizations reached by inductive inference.[24] From a methodological point of view, therefore, dogmatic and historical theology needed each other just as much as the empiricists and dogmatists in Galen's medical treatises: the inquiring mind was supposed to move back and forth between the general and the particular. Clearly, in this line of reasoning, "dogmatic" had nothing to do with blind faith or succumbing to authority: dogmatic reasoning was just as indispensable an element of learning as the study of particulars.[25]

Quintilian's influence in turn is visible in seventeenth-century encyclopedia entries that sharply distinguished between *philosophia dogmatica* and *philosophia elenctica*. Apart from the terminology being reminiscent of Quintilian, the very notion of dogmatic philosophy drew on Quintilian's connection between the dogmatic and the didactic. Johann Heinrich Alsted's encyclopedia of 1630 even used "dogmatic" and "didactic" as almost interchangeable terms.[26] It is perhaps no coincidence that this Quintilian-

---

[20] Galen, *On the Properties of Foodstuffs*, trans. Owen Powell (Cambridge: Cambridge University Press, 2003), 29–30 (*Alim. fac.* I, 1).

[21] Galen, *Method of Medicine*, trans. Ian Johnston and G. H. R. Horsley (Cambridge, MA: Harvard University Press, 2011), 371, 183, 283 (*MM*, IV.244K, II.117K, III.184K).

[22] Herberger, *Dogmatik*, 100.–1.

[23] Filser, *Dogma*, 382.

[24] On the connotations of *historia* in this period, see Gianna Pomata and Nancy G. Siraisi (eds.), *Historia: Empiricism and Erudition in Early Modern Europe* (Cambridge, MA: MIT Press, 2005).

[25] This is evident also from Leibniz's distinction between *medicina dogmatica* and *medicina autoritate nixa*: authority-based medicine was something very different from dogmatic medicine. Quoted in Herberger, *Dogmatik*, 4, 308.

[26] Ibid., 294–5.

style argument was put forward at a time that also witnessed the rise of experimental research practices. By presenting dogmatism as the most appropriate "method of teaching and learning" (*methodus docendi et discendi*),[27] Alsted and his colleagues created room for the idea that dogmatic ways of reasoning are appropriate in the classroom, but not in the laboratory or the field.

* * *

If anywhere, it was in seventeenth-century England that this idea took root.[28] In an emerging culture of experimental science, more inclined to unraveling nature's secrets with telescopes and thermometers than repeating the classic wisdom of Aristotelian natural philosophy, the adjective "dogmatic" became a pejorative term for those who still preferred textbook wisdom over experimental science. Consequently, for the first time in its history, dogmatism came to be regarded as a vice, that is, a trait of character or "temper of mind" detrimental to the pursuit of true learning.[29] Thomas Hobbes, for instance, presented *mathematici* and *dogmatici* not merely as "two sorts of men" but also as incarnations of virtue and vice, respectively. While he depicted mathematicians as humble and peaceable scholars, he portrayed their opponents, the dogmatists, as quasi-scholars who "are imperfectly learned, and with passion press to have their opinions pass everywhere for truth." On top of that, Hobbes claimed that *dogmatici* "take up maxims from their education, and from the authority of men, or of custom, and take the habitual discourse of the tongue for ratiocination."[30] Hobbes' dogmatists, in other words, were not only too much enslaved by their passions to be able to engage in serious scholarly work but also made themselves guilty of appealing to authority, while mistaking conventional wisdom for established truth.

A similar picture of unrestrained passion and stubborn adherence to established truth standing in the way of scholarly progress was painted by Joseph Glanvill and Thomas Sprat, the two tireless apologists of the Royal Society. In his programmatically titled book, *The Vanity of Dogmatizing* (1661), Glanvill emphasized the need for careful, conscientious research by offering

---

[27] Ibid., 294.
[28] This section is indebted to Sorana Corneanu's conference paper, "Dogmatism and Imagination: The Making of an Early Modern Epistemic Vice," delivered at Leiden University in January 2018.
[29] Tho[mas] Sprat, *The History of the Royal-Society of London, for the Improving of Natural Knowledge* (London: J. Martyn, 1667), 33.
[30] Thomas Hobbes, "The Elements of Law" (1640), in *Three-Text Edition of Thomas Hobbes's Political Theory: The Elements of Law, De cive, and Leviathan*, trans. Deborah Baumgold (Cambridge: Cambridge University Press, 2017), 3–548, at 125.

a grim picture of humans being slaves of passion, prejudice, and ignorance. Given that this condition rendered any claim to knowledge implausible, dogmatists made themselves guilty of hubris: "*Confidence* is arrogance, and *Dogmatizing* unreasonable presuming."[31] Or as Glanvill put it in his essay, "Against Confidence in Philosophy" (1676):

> *Dogmatizing* in things uncertain, doth commonly inhabit with *untamed Passions*, and is usually maintain'd upon the *obstinacy* of an *ungovern'd* Spirit. For one of the first Rules in the *Art* of *Self-Government* is, to be *modest* in Opinions . . . Tis *Pride*, and *Presumption* of ones self that causeth such forwardness and assurance; and where those *reign*, there is neither *Virtue* nor *Reason*; No *regular Government*, but a miserable *Tyranny* of *Passion* and *Self-will*.[32]

These three sentences contain what one might call a "regimen of mind": an entire program of shaping the self by cultivating virtues of modesty in the hope of thereby constraining the power of passions and prejudices that prevent human beings from acquiring real knowledge of the world.[33]

Sprat, likewise, saw dogmatism as a habit of mind that stifled all desire for knowledge: "It makes men give over, and believe that they are satisfi'd, too soon. This is of very ill consequence: For thereby mens industry will be slackned, and all the motives to any farther pursuit taken away."[34] If this defined dogmatism as a problem of premature closure—people thinking they have answers without even having begun exploring the questions— Sprat also associated dogmatism with a habitual unwillingness to learn from others and be corrected if needed. Such a habit was not exactly beneficial to cooperative research of the kind practiced in the Royal Society. This led Sprat to conclude that as long as people are "immovable in their opinions" and "prone to undervalue other mens labours," they are lacking "the Character of a True Philosopher."[35] Although this twofold critique shows that there were

---

[31] Jos[eph] Glanvill, *The Vanity of Dogmatizing: or Confidence in Opinions Manifested in a Discourse of the Shortness and Uncertainty of Our Knowledge, and Its Causes* . . . (London: Henry Eversden, 1661), unpaginated preface.

[32] Joseph Glanvill, "Against Confidence in Philosophy, and Matters of Speculation," in Glanvill, *Essays on Several Important Subjects in Philosophy and Religion* (London: John Baker, 1676), 1–33, at 30.

[33] Sorana Corneanu, *Regimens of the Mind: Boyle, Locke, and the Early Modern Cultura Animi Tradition* (Chicago: University of Chicago Press, 2011); Matthew L. Jones, *The Good Life in the Scientific Revolution: Descartes, Pascal, Leibniz, and the Cultivation of Virtue* (Chicago: University of Chicago Press, 2006).

[34] Sprat, *History*, 32.

[35] Ibid., 33, 34.

several grounds on which dogmatism could be construed as a scholarly vice, most important for our purposes is the category of vice as such. For Hobbes, Glanvill, Sprat, and others, the adjective "dogmatic" no longer applied to schools or methods; it denoted a *habit of mind* detrimental to serious inquiry.

* * *

This new conceptualization provided very influential, even if older meanings of the term did not die out. By the eighteenth century, the notion of dogmatism as a vice, scholarly or otherwise, had firmly established itself. In his popular logic textbook of 1726, Isaac Watts almost literally echoed Sprat and Glanvill in stating that "the *Dogmatist* is in haste to believe something; he can't keep himself long enough in Suspence, till some bright and convincing Evidence appear on one Side; but throws himself casually into the Sentiments of one Party or another, and then he will hear no Argument to the contrary." Dogmatism, then, was a "humour" or "temper of mind," which Watts believed was prevalent especially among "the lower Rank of People both in learned and in vulgar Life."[36] None of these claims were original: the idea that dogmatism reigned especially among the unenlightened can be found in many variants across Europe in the eighteenth century.[37]

Although it would be wrong to assume that eighteenth-century authors expected such unenlightened habits to manifest themselves with particular force in the church, it is worth observing that dogmatism became increasingly associated with rigid church doctrine and abusive ecclesial authority. Judging by the entry "Dogmatique" in the *Encyclopédie* (28 vols., 1751–72) of Denis Diderot and Jean le Rond d'Alembert, medical dogmatism still was a matter of greater concern (taking up four times as many words) than theological dogmatism.[38] Other entries, however, illustrate that dogmatism invoked the images of a fanatical John Calvin who allowed Michael Servetus to be burned at the stake and of traumatic events like the Wars of Religion, which the entry on "Christianisme" attributed to a "dogmatic spirit . . . innate in Christianity."[39] Voltaire, likewise, held a Calvinist *esprit dogmatique* responsible for the Wars

---

[36] Isaac Watts, *Logick: or, the Right Use of Reason in the Enquiry after Truth . . .* 4th ed. (London: Emanuel Matthews, 1731), 211, 209, 210.

[37] See, for example, David Hume, "Dialogues Concerning Natural Religion" (1779), in Hume, *Dialogues Concerning Natural Religion and Other Writings*, ed. Dorothy Coleman (Cambridge: Cambridge University Press, 2007), 1–102, at 32 (III.7).

[38] "Dogmatique," in *Encyclopédie, ou dictionnaire raisonné des sciences, des arts et des métiers*, vol. 5 (Paris: Briasson et al., 1755), 12–3.

[39] "Dogmatiser," ibid., 13; "Christianisme," in *Encyclopédie, ou dictionnaire raisonné des sciences, des arts et des métiers*, vol. 3 (Paris: Briasson et al., 1753), 381–7, at 384.

of Religion.[40] An even clearer illustration of dogmatism acquiring connotations of religious zealotry can be found in Jean-Jacques Rousseau's *Letters Written From the Mountain* (1762). Although Rousseau was prepared to admit that "true Christianity is an institution of peace," he noted that the sort of religion preached from pulpits in France and Switzerland alike amounted to a "dogmatic or theological Christianity," which "by the multitude and obscurity of its dogmas and above all by the obligation to accept them" created near-permanent conflict among its adherents. From Rousseau's point of view, therefore, "dogmatic Christianity" was unable to bring peace on earth.[41] Although we will argue in Chapter 4 that such religious connotations of "dogmatism" would reach their high point only in the 1870s, the groundwork for this understanding of the term was laid in eighteenth-century France.

All this implies that the adjective "dogmatic" had quite a career before Kant. Apart from the two ancient meanings of the term, represented by Galen and Quintilian and echoed by sixteenth- and seventeenth-century authors alike, there were Royal Society apologists who already by the 1660s attacked "the vanity of dogmatizing" and French critics of revealed religion, a century later, who associated dogmatism with ecclesial authority and religious intolerance. What, then, was new in Kant's 1781 assault on dogmatism?

* * *

Eisler's claim that Kant was responsible for turning the adjective into a noun does not hold. In the 1770s, Kant's fellow-philosopher Christoph Meiners had already waged an attack on dogmatism.[42] In French (not to mention earlier uses in the classical languages), the term "dogmatisme" even goes back to Montaigne's *Essays*.[43] As early as 1611, Randle Cotgrave had included it in his French-English dictionary.[44] Although this does not detract anything from Kant's importance, it does suggest that Kant popularized rather than invented

---

[40] Voltaire, *Essay sur l'histoire générale, et sur les moeurs et l'esprit des nations, depuis Charlemagne jusqu'à nos jours*, vol. 6 ([The Hague]: [J. Néaulme], 1757), 281, 282.

[41] Jean-Jacques Rousseau, "Letters Written from the Mountain" (1764), in Rousseau, *Letter to Beaumont, Letters Written from the Mountain, and Related Writings*, trans. Christopher Kelly and Judith R. Bush (Hanover: University Press of New England, 2001), 131–306, at 148, 149.

[42] [Christoph Meiners], *Revision der Philosophie*, vol. 1 (Göttingen: Johann Christian Dieterich, 1772), 38, 87, 89 134; Meiners, *Versuch über die Religionsgeschichte der ältesten Völker besonders der Egyptier* (Göttingen: Johann Christian Dieterich, 1775), 188. Context is provided in Walther Ch. Zimmerli, "'Schwere Rüstung' des Dogmatismus und 'anwendbare Eklektik': J. G. H. Feder und die Göttinger Philosophie im ausgehenden 18. Jahrhundert," *Studia Leibnitiana* 15, no. 1 (1983): 58–71.

[43] Montaigne, *Essays*, vol. 2, 268.

[44] Randle Cotgrave, *A Dictionarie of the French and English Tongues* (London: Adam Islip, 1611), s.v. dogmatisme.

the "ism" ending. Similarly, Kant covered familiar ground in arguing that dogmatism is not only a way of doing philosophy but also a corresponding habit of mind. If it is dogmatic to philosophize "without an antecedent critique of [reason's] own capacity," then the dogmatist, according to Kant, is an unduly "confident," "self-conceited," and "uncritical" type of thinker.[45] Insofar as this amounted to saying that dogmatists are too self-assured and too quickly satisfied, Kant accused his opponents of vices similar to those disparaged by Sprat and Glanvill. Much the same applies to Kant's polemical uses of the term, which at times bordered on ridicule ("If one sees the dogmatist step forward with ten proofs, one can be sure that he has none at all").[46] When a German reviewer, in response to passages like this one, complained that Kant used dogmatism as an invective, with the apparent aim of "stigmatizing" colleagues past and present, he put his finger on a rhetorical technique that scholars had been practicing already since the seventeenth century.[47]

If Kant's first *Critique* nonetheless marks a watershed in the history of dogmatism, it does so for two reasons. The first is that Kant introduced a new conceptual antithesis, between *Dogmatismus* and *Kritik*. Although this pair of terms was grafted on older distinctions, such as the age-old contrast between skeptic and dogmatic modes of philosophy, Kant first and foremost depicted dogmatism as the naïve, unreflective, uncritical opposite of "critical" philosophy. The defining difference between the two was that dogmatists, according to Kant, refuse to reflect on the conditions of philosophical reasoning, whereas critical philosophers deserve their name by practicing "a critique of the faculty of human reason in general, in respect of all the cognitions after which reason might strive . . . the possibility or impossibility of a metaphysics in general, and the determination of its sources, as well as its extent and boundaries."[48] For Kant, then, dogmatism was the principal other of his own, critical project—which may explain the condescending tone in which he spoke about "dogmatic slumber," "sweet dogmatic dreams," and dogmatic

---

[45] Immanuel Kant, *Critique of Pure Reason*, trans. Paul Guyer (Cambridge: Cambridge University Press, 1998), 119 (Bxxxv), 139 (B7), 652 (A757/B785), 658 (A768/B796). See also Immanuel Kant, *Critique of Practical Reason*, trans. Mary Gregor (Cambridge: Cambridge University Press, 1997), 86 (5:103).

[46] Kant, *Critique of Pure Reason*, 668 (A789/B817).

[47] Johann August Eberhard, "Über die Schranken der menschlichen Erkenntnis" (1789), in Immanuel Kant, *Der Streit mit Johann August Eberhard*, ed. Marion Lauschke and Manfred Zahn (Hamburg: Felix Meiner, 1998), 3–15, at 4. On Kant's and Eberhard's conflicting views of dogmatism, see Manfred Gawlina, *Das Medusenhaupt der Kritik: Die Kontroverse zwischen Immanuel Kant und Johann August Eberhard* (Berlin: Walter de Gruyter, 1996), 107–11.

[48] Kant, *Critique of Pure Reason*, 101 (Axii).

"poison" doing its dirty work.[49] Although there is little evidence that Kant drew on existing notions of critique as developed in the seventeenth and eighteenth centuries, it is safe to assume that Kant's contrast between dogmatism and critique hit a chord partly because it brought together, in one pair of words, a centuries-old vice and an intellectual aspiration that, however differently interpreted, was shared widely among scholars in Enlightenment Europe.[50]

Adding to the appeal of this contrast was a second feature of Kant's *Dogmatismus*: he portrayed it as belonging to a foregone era. Although Kant was not the first to argue that dogmatism should be overcome—already in 1620, Francis Bacon had claimed that bees were more useful insects than the ants (*empirici*) and spiders (*dogmatici*) that so far had populated the Republic of Letters[51]—no one prior to Kant had as resolutely presented dogmatism as a relic from the past as the Königsberg philosopher did in 1781. This is perhaps best visible in Kant's three-stage model, according to which critical philosophy replaced skepticism as practiced by Hume, which in its turn had succeeded dogmatism as represented by Leibniz and Wolff. Comparing these three stages in the evolution of European philosophy to human phases of maturation, Kant argued: "The first step in matters of pure reason, which characterizes its childhood, is *dogmatic*. The . . . second step is *skeptical*, and gives evidence of the caution of the power of judgment sharpened by experience. Now, however, a third step is still necessary . . .; this is not the censorship but the *critique* of pure reason."[52] This narrative of progress explains why Kant endowed the term *Dogmatismus* with connotations of obsoleteness and old-fashionedness. Time and again, he referred to "old worm-eaten *dogmatism*" or the "old dogmatic procedure of philosophy," thereby suggesting that dogmatism was no longer at home in modern philosophy.[53] As we shall see in Chapter 3, this would become a popular line of reasoning among nineteenth-century critics of dogmatism.

* * *

---

[49] Immanuel Kant, *Prolegomena to Any Future Metaphysics That Will Be Able to Come Forward as Science*, trans. Gary Hatfield (Cambridge: Cambridge University Press, 1997), 10 (4:260); Kant, *Critique of Pure Reason*, 652 (A757/B785), 651 (A755/B783). On the dogmatic slumber metaphor, see Abraham Anderson, *Kant, Hume, and the Interruption of Dogmatic Slumber* (Oxford: Oxford University Press, 2020).

[50] J. Colin McQuillan, *Immanuel Kant: The Very Idea of a Critique of Pure Reason* (Evanston: Northwestern University Press, 2016), 3–20, esp. 17; Giorgio Tonelli, "'Critique' and Related Terms Prior to Kant: A Historical Survey," *Kant-Studien* 69 (1978): 119–48.

[51] Francis Bacon, *The New Organon*, ed. Lisa Jardine and Michael Silverthorne (Cambridge: Cambridge University Press, 2000), 79 (I, xcv).

[52] Kant, *Critique of Pure Reason*, 654 (A761/B789).

[53] Ibid., 100 (Ax); Kant, *Critique of Practical Reason*, 8 (5:10).

Although Eisler, the Viennese dictionary compiler, ignored most of the history traced in this chapter, he was right to highlight Kant's considerable influence on what later generations of German philosophers understood dogmatism to mean. In various ways, Idealist philosophers from Fichte to Hegel appropriated and reworked Kant's conceptual contrast between criticism and dogmatism.[54] Even Friedrich Wilhelm Joseph Schelling, whose *Philosophical Letters on Dogmatism and Criticism* (1795) made a case for both "isms" being viable options, agreed with Kant that it was wrong to develop a philosophical position blindly, "without any preceding investigation of the cognitive faculty."[55] Something similar applies to neo-Kantian philosophers, whose influence was particularly strong in Germany, France, and Italy. When Italy's leading nineteenth-century neo-Kantian, Carlo Cantoni, reviewed the field of moral philosophy in the 1870s, he saw threats of dogmatism lurking almost everywhere.[56]

Philosophers, however, were not alone in distancing themselves from dogmatism. As the next chapters will make clear, accusations of dogmatism were made across the academic spectrum, by scientists and humanities scholars alike. Interestingly, they frequently did so along the lines explored in this opening chapter. More often than not, nineteenth- and twentieth-century authors drew on well-established resources in depicting dogmatism as a scientific method, in framing it as a vicious habit of mind, or in treating it as a remnant from a pre-critical era. The history of dogmatism up until Kant, in other words, served as a repertoire from which later generations, intentionally or otherwise, would copiously draw.

---

[54] On which, see, briefly, Nieke, "Dogmatismus," 277–8.

[55] Friedrich Wilhelm Joseph Schelling, "Philosophical Letters on Dogmatism and Criticism" (1795), in Schelling, *The Unconditional in Human Knowledge: Four Early Essays (1794–1796)*, trans. Fritz Marti (Lewisburg: Bucknell University Press, 1980), 156–96, at 169.

[56] Carlo Cantoni, *Corso elementare di filosofia*, vol. 2, 4th ed. (Milan: Ulrico Hoepli, 1886), passim.

3

A Relic from the Past
Dogmatism in the Age of Progress

I n describing Wolffian metaphysics as "old worm-eaten dogmatism," Kant used a powerful metaphor. *Wurmstichig* was an adjective typically used for old furniture, half destroyed by wood-boring beetle larvae, or metaphorically applied to outmoded arrangements "from which the spirit has long fled and which the reason of this age has long condemned."[1] If anything, the metaphor conveyed that dogmatism was *veraltet*, outdated, or old-fashioned. Although the phrase did not become as proverbial as Kant's "dogmatic slumber"— nineteenth-century authors used it almost exclusively in relation to Kant himself—it was an early expression of what in the decades following the publication of the *Critique of Pure Reason* became a dominant connotation of the term. Dogmatism, wrote a German book reviewer in 1814, had collapsed into ruins: once a proud edifice, it had now become a symbol of times past.[2]

Views like this were typical of a century that was an age of progress, scientifically and otherwise, as well as an age of historicism—that is, a time in which changes in science or society were typically framed in developmental terms, as next steps in long processes of gradual improvement.[3] It was this

---

[1] N. N., *Die neue Zeit: Von einem alten Constituonellen*, vol. 11 (Stuttgart: Friedrich Henne, 1832), 288.

[2] N. N., review of *Aphorismen zur Erneuerung des kirchlichen Lebens im protestantischen Deutschland* [II], *Allgemeine Literatur-Zeitung* (1814), 705–10, at 706.

[3] Key studies of historicism so defined are John Edward Toews, *Becoming Historical: Cultural Reformation and Public Memory in Early Nineteenth-Century Berlin* (Cambridge: Cambridge

interpretive template that led many authors to echo Kant in arguing that dogmatism had become a thing of the past, out of place in a so-called modern era. As we will see, this way of contrasting the new and the old—a rhetorical figure that can be traced back to Renaissance polemics about *modernitas* and *antiquitas*[4]—had effects well beyond the representation of, say, scholastic philosophy in the supposedly "dark" Middle Ages.[5] The polemical edge of this template became most evident when present-day scholars were accused of obstructing scientific progress. Authors charged with dogmatism were denied a place in the present: they were relegated to a "prescientific" or "precritical" past because of their perceived old-fashioned views. In a culture where belief in progress was deeply ingrained in the scientific imagination, this implied that charges of dogmatism were potentially more devastating than accusations of inaccuracy or oversight. If dogmatism was a relic from the past, then dogmatic scholars were living anachronisms—more at home in a museum than in a laboratory.

If this chapter examines the term's archaic connotations, the next one will survey the ecclesial connotations that dogmatism acquired at a time when science and religion came to be seen as antagonistic powers. These chapters form a diptych insofar as they cover two of the most prominent layers of meaning that dogmatism had for nineteenth-century scholars— with a third one, that of dogmatism as a vice, implied in both of them. As shown in Chapter 2, none of this was new: all three had antecedents in the seventeenth and eighteenth centuries. However, at a time when scientists liked to stylize themselves as men of virtue, when progress became central to the self-understanding of almost every scholarly field, and when the topic of "science and religion" provoked the most emotional responses, these layers of meaning acquired greater significance than they had enjoyed before.

*   *   *

If there is one genre testifying to the power of nineteenth-century visions of progress, it is the history of science books like William Whewell's *History of the Inductive Sciences* (3 vols., 1837). A longtime master of Trinity College,

---

University Press, 2004) and Mark Bevir (ed.), *Historicism and the Human Sciences in Victorian Britain* (Cambridge: Cambridge University Press, 2017).

[4] Charles Trinkaus, "*Antiquitas* Versus *Modernitas*: An Italian Humanist Polemic and Its Resonance," *Journal of the History of Ideas* 48, no. 1 (1987): 11–21.

[5] On the image of scholasticism in modern views of medieval philosophy, see Catherine König-Pralong, *Médiévisme philosophique et raison moderne: de Pierre Bayle à Ernest Renan* (Paris: J. Vrin, 2016) and Sjang ten Hagen, "Scholasticism as a Scholarly Vice Term: From the Middle Ages to the Twenty-First Century" (forthcoming).

Cambridge, Whewell is known for having coined the word "scientist" in 1834. Despite initial resistance, the term stuck because it allowed modern practitioners of science to distinguish themselves from early modern men of science, commonly known as natural philosophers.[6] The book *History of the Inductive Sciences*, likewise, testifies to Whewell's belief that nineteenth-century science had advanced considerably over the scholarly wisdom of previous centuries. Drawing on canonical Enlightenment texts like d'Alembert and Diderot's *Encyclopédie*, Whewell's book was a triumphant history of "the progress of physical science in modern times," full of praise for experimentalists like Galileo Galilei and Robert Boyle as well as for Francis Bacon, whose "Great Reform of Philosophy and Method" Whewell presented as a vision with which nineteenth-century scientists could still identify.[7]

Dogmatism appeared in Whewell's book as the very opposite of progress. First and foremost, the term was applied to the Middle Ages, which Whewell regarded as a "stationary period," in which men of learning had suffered from a host of "defects and errors." Their lack of empirical zeal was evident from their enthusiasm for speculation, just as their veneration of ancient authorities like Aristotle testified to their "want of courage and originality."[8] In Whewell's understanding of dogmatism, this reliance on the wisdom of the past was a defining element. "Men forgot, or feared, to consult nature, to seek for new truths, to do what the great discoverers of other times had done; they were content to consult libraries, to study and defend old opinions . . ." Consequently, modern science had been able to emerge only when men of learning had abandoned "their blind admiration for the ancients, and were disposed to cast away also their passive obedience to the ancient system of doctrines."[9]

If this suggests that dogmatism was a yoke that men of science had cast off successfully in the so-called Scientific Revolution (another historiographical category that Whewell helped establish),[10] it is important to add that, in Whewell's view of things, the victory of scientific research over dogmatic thinking had never been complete. Near the end of his *History* as well as in

[6] Sydney Ross, "Scientist: The Story of a Word," *Annals of Science* 18, no. 2 (1962): 65–85, at 71–2.
[7] William Whewell, *History of the Inductive Sciences, from the Earliest to the Present Times*, vol. 1 (London: John W. Parker, 1837), 329, 243, vii, viii.
[8] Ibid., 186, 235, 236, 312.
[9] Ibid., 312, 356. Although ecclesial connotations were largely absent from his *History*, Whewell's sequel project, *The Philosophy of the Inductive Sciences*, attributed dogmatic inclinations to medieval doctors of the church who "put forth to control men's opinions upon all subjects," while imposing speculative theories upon them "with the imperative tone of rules of conduct and faith." *The Philosophy of the Inductive Sciences, Founded upon Their History*, vol. 2 (London: John W. Parker, 1840), 314, 306. We will explore these and other ecclesial connotations in Chapter 4.
[10] H. F. Cohen, *The Scientific Revolution: A Historiographical Inquiry* (Chicago: University of Chicago Press, 1994), 27–39.

several later publications, Whewell pointed out that the "spirit of dogmatism" had reemerged in seventeenth-century Italy, among clerical opponents of Galilei's heliocentrism, as well as in England, where Thomas Hobbes—the philosopher whom we encountered earlier as a critic of *dogmatici*—had displayed "the most extravagant arrogance, ignorance, and dogmatism which can be imagined."[11] In 1852, Whewell noted that the philosopher Jeremy Bentham, who had died only twenty years earlier, had "habitually indulge[d]" in dogmatism.[12] The vice even manifested itself among living geologists, judging by Whewell's survey of the nineteenth-century dispute between catastrophists and uniformitarians. Writing in the present tense, Whewell accused the former of a dogmatism matched only by the skepticism of the latter.[13] Apparently, the evil of dogmatism had not disappeared with the dawn of the modern age: even scientists (to use Whewell's neologism) could relapse into this old error.

Arguably, Whewell's most enduring legacy was his grand historical narrative, which secured dogmatism a reputation as a typically medieval vice. In this historical scheme, dogmatism was a remnant of the past insofar as it privileged the bookish knowledge of ancient authorities over empirical investigations of nature. In addition, however, the narrative offered scholars a template for interpreting more recent violations of their own standards as historical setbacks. More specifically, it provided them with a tool for relegating supposedly dogmatic opponents into the darkness of a medieval past. In an age marveling at the progress of science, was there a more serious accusation than the insinuation of having a premodern mindset?

* * *

Whewell's *History* set the tone for many subsequent history of science titles, monodisciplinary histories included. Together with Auguste Comte, whose *Course of Positive Philosophy* (6 vols., 1830–42) presented a related but distinct story of progress, Whewell shaped the narrative of science coming of age, similar to how Kant had done this for the field of philosophy.[14] With or without mentioning his name, many an author adopted Whewell's storyline of dogmatism receding into the past due to "the advance of physical knowledge."[15]

---

[11] Whewell, *History*, vol. 1, 398; William Whewell, *Lectures on the Moral Philosophy in England*, vol. 1 (John W. Parker and Son, 1852), 28.

[12] Whewell, *Lectures*, vol. 1, 255.

[13] Whewell, *Philosophy*, vol. 1, xxxvi.

[14] Rachel Laudan, "Histories of Sciences and Their Uses: A Review to 1913," *History of Science* 31, no. 1 (1993): 1–34, esp. 15–20.

[15] Whewell, *History*, vol. 1, 376.

An 1843 history of chemistry, for instance, begrudged "the most arrogant dogmatism" of early modern alchemists—an image that contrasted nicely with that of modern experimental chemistry.[16] Similarly, Julius Sachs' history of botany explained how Matthias Jacob Schleiden, one of the originators of cell theory, had broken the power of "dogmatic, scholastic, trivial, and uncritical" botany as it had existed "back then."[17] The plot proved applicable to the history of mathematics, too. This is how, near the end of the century, Florian Cajori described the Scientific Revolution:

> The pulse and pace of the world began to quicken. Men's minds became less servile; they became clearer and stronger. . . . Dogmatism was attacked; there arose a long struggle with the authority of the Church and the established schools of philosophy. . . . Thus, by slow degrees, the minds of men were cut adrift from their old scholastic moorings and sent forth on the wide sea of scientific inquiry, to discover new islands and continents of truths.[18]

Stories of new science trumping old dogmatism also circulated in a more popular form. In *A Short History of Natural Science* (1876), Arabella Buckley—an author of whom Charles Darwin once said that she treated evolution "with much dexterity and truthfulness"—contrasted the rise of modern science with the "dogmatism of the Middle Ages."[19] Likewise, Robert Routledge told his readers that opposition to Copernicus' astronomy in sixteenth-century Europe had been fueled by "the dogmatism of the old philosophy."[20] Like their academic equivalents, popular history of science books were premised on the assumption that history progressed from darkness to light, with dogmatism serving as an old vice that modern science had virtuously overcome.

In passing, it is worth noting that Francis Bacon, whom Whewell greatly admired "as the Hero of the revolution in scientific method," was frequently

---

[16] Ferd[inand] Hoefer, *Histoire de la chimie depuis les temps les plus reculés jusqu'à notre époque*, vol. 2 (Paris: L. Hachette, 1843), 338.

[17] Julius Sachs, *Geschichte der Botanik vom 16. Jahrhundert bis 1860* (Munich: R. Oldenbourg, 1875), 204.

[18] Florian Cajori, *A History of Mathematics* (New York: Macmillan and Co., 1894), 138–9.

[19] Charles Darwin to Arabella Buckley, November 14, 1880, in Frederick Burkhardt et al. (eds.), *The Correspondence of Charles Darwin*, vol. 28 (Cambridge: Cambridge University Press, 2021), 79; Arabella B. Buckley, *A Short History of Natural Science and of the Progress of Discovery from the Time of the Greeks to the Present Day: For the Use of Schools and Young Persons* (London: John Murray, 1876), 63.

[20] Robert Routledge, *A Popular History of Science* (London: George Routledge and Sons, 1881), 84.

assigned a key role in this process.[21] Not afraid of mixing metaphors, a German history of biology book presented Bacon as "the new light that with the force of its rays enlightened the medieval darkness, shattering the ice crust of dogmatism."[22] While Buckley echoed Whewell in claiming that Bacon had inaugurated "the true method of studying Science," Routledge devoted a whole chapter to the man who had brought about "the final overthrow" of scholastic dogmatism—complete with a portrait of Bacon, a picture of his statue in Westminster Abbey, and a eulogy in verse penned by Abraham Cowley:

> From these and all long errors of the way,
> In which our wandering predecessors went,
> And, like the old Hebrews, many years did stray
> In deserts but of small extent,—
> Bacon, like Moses, led us forth at last.[23]

Lest these examples suggest that everyone adopted Whewell's template, there were other voices, too. As we shall see in Chapter 6, Comte's story of progress was markedly different from Whewell's in that it did not abandon dogmatism but culminated in a dogmatic stage—whereby dogmatic thinking was presented as an aspiration rather than a vice. Also, when it came to socializing students into the practice of science, it was not uncommon for educators to sympathize with approaches that were dogmatic in the old sense of presenting a body of scholarly knowledge in a systematic, student-friendly manner (Chapter 2). Historical accounts, however, mostly followed Whewell in depicting dogmatism as a superseded stage in the history of science.

* * *

To what extent did nineteenth-century scientists also follow Whewell in presenting modern-day dogmatists—colleagues, that is, whom they perceived as dogmatic—as anomalies in a story of progress? If it was true, as an 1877 article in *Nature* maintained, that "the domain of dogmatic belief

---

[21] Whewell, *Philosophy*, 392. Whewell has been described as "Bacon's arch-admirer": Antonio Pérez-Ramos, "Bacon's Legacy," in Marku Peltonen (ed.), *The Cambridge Companion to Bacon* (Cambridge: Cambridge University Press, 2006), 311–34, at 323.

[22] G. A. Erdmann, *Geschichte der Entwicklung und Methodik der biologischen Naturwissenschaften (Zoologie und Botanik)* . . . (Kassel: Theodor Fischer, 1887), 20.

[23] Buckley, *Short History*, 103; Routledge, *Popular History*, 126, 142, quoting A. Cowley, "To the Royal Society," in Tho[mas] Sprat, *The History of the Royal-Society of London, for the Improving of Natural Knowledge* (London: J. Martyn, 1667), unpaginated front matter.

is lessened year after year in favour of objective knowledge which is based upon facts," one would not expect to find dogmatists at nineteenth-century universities.[24] However, as the same *Nature* article continued in a tone of worry, there was actually no lack of scholars whose subjective beliefs and fanciful hypotheses betrayed the principles of Baconian science. Dogmatists, likewise, could be found among the living just as easily as among the dead. In the field of chemistry, for example, it was not just the early modern phlogiston theory that counted as "petrified dogma."[25] According to a German history of chemistry book, written shortly after the Franco-Prussian War (1870–1), many French chemists were in the habit of uncritically embracing fossilized dogmas: "Probably at no other point in time dogma was more welcomed, more readily believed, than right now. Especially the French school [*Richtung*] demonstrates how eagerly systems that are presented as finished, incapable of further development, are being taken up."[26] Although this argument was not free from nationalist overtones (a theme to which we will return in Chapter 5), the Swiss-born anatomist Wilhelm His agreed that dogmatists had anything but died out. In the *Proceedings of the Royal Society of Edinburgh* (1888), he observed:

> In our scientific development we have not all travelled the same way. Many scientific men follow what we may call the dogmatic or scholastic way. . . . Strong dogmatists are not only partial in adopting or rejecting observations of others, but they are also partial in their own work. They observe natural facts, not as they present themselves, but as they should be seen in the light of the dogma. . . . It would be easy to point out many instances of such partialities in actual text-books, as well as in actual monographs.[27]

It was possible, of course, to accept modern-day dogmatism as a matter of fact. The historian of physics Ferdinand Rosenberger came close to such a position when he presented a quasi-cyclical model according to which "times of critical resignation and hopeful trust in the power of the human mind continuously alternate." In this scheme of things, dogmatism would soon be displaced by critical or skeptical thinking—but only momentarily, not once

---

[24] N. N., "The German Association at Munich," *Nature* 16, no. 414 (1877): 491–2, at 492.

[25] Ernst von Meyer, *Geschichte der Chemie von den ältesten Zeiten bis zur Gegenwart: zugleich eine Einführung in das Studium der Chemie* (Leipzig: Veit & Comp., 1889), 128.

[26] Albrecht Rau, *Die Entwicklung der modernen Chemie* (Braunschweig: Vieweg und Sohn, 1879), 99.

[27] Wilhelm His, "On the Principles of Animal Morphology: Letter to Mr John Murray," *Proceedings of the Royal Society of Edinburgh* 15 (1888): 287–98, at 288–9.

and for all.[28] More widely accepted, however, was the Whewellian view that dogmatism was an anomaly in an era of inductive science. Not only was this view best compatible with a robust faith in the progress of science, but it also allowed for effective polemics: it offered scholars a template for depicting dogmatists as out of joint with modern times.

German philosophy in the 1870s is a case in point.[29] Although the field was not notably indebted to Whewell, Kant's presence was such that philosophers almost without exception associated dogmatism with a mode of thinking that by the end of the eighteenth century had been replaced by Kantian criticism. History of philosophy textbooks testified to this view when they presented "the time of empiricism, dogmatism, and skepticism" as lasting from René Descartes to David Hume, whose death in 1776 had marked a transition to "the time of Kantian criticism."[30] Similarly, another textbook claimed that philosophy had ascended from a dogmatic stage to a critical one: "Spinoza reigned over the first, Kant over the second era of this philosophy; the former completed dogmatism, the latter founded criticism."[31] From this perspective, dogmatism was simultaneously a vice (a naïve lack of attention to the conditions of human knowledge) and a relic from the past. In Kantian terminology, it was "worm-rotten thinking." This explains, on the one hand, why textbook authors like Kuno Fischer had little positive to say about colleagues whom they saw succumbing to dogmatism. "These dogmatists of today, who take pride in ignoring Kant and Fichte and march in parade style through pre-Kantian theories of materialism and supernaturalism claim in vain that they are philosophers: these good chaps know and feel nothing of the heroic power of this philosophical age. . . ."[32] On the other hand, this periodization scheme gave charges of dogmatism a sharp polemical edge. To the extent that the vice was typical of premodern times, accusations of dogmatism amounted to expulsion from the present.

In the so-called Pessimism Controversy—a protracted debate on the merits of Arthur Schopenhauer's and Eduard von Hartmann's grim philosophies of life—German philosophers did not hesitate to make this implication explicit. "What was forgivable before Kant, vain dogmatizing," said one of Hartmann's

---

[28] Ferd[inand] Rosenberger, *Die Geschichte der Physik in Grundzügen* . . ., vol. 3 (Braunschweig: Friedrich Vieweg und Sohn, 1887–90), 319.

[29] The remainder of this section draws on Caroline Schep and Herman Paul, "Denial of Coevalness: Charges of Dogmatism in the Nineteenth-Century Humanities," *History of European Ideas* 48, no. 6 (2022): 778–94.

[30] Friedrich Ueberweg, *Grundriss der Geschichte der Philosophie von Thales bis auf die Gegenwart*, vol. 3 (Berlin: E. S. Mittler & Sohn, 1866), 1.

[31] Kuno Fischer, *Vorlesungen über Geschichte der neueren Philosophie*, vol. 1 (Stuttgart: C. P. Scheitlin, 1852), viii.

[32] Ibid., ix.

opponents, "is unforgivable after Kant. May all the Hartmanns at long last learn as much from the clear words of the clear Königsberg thinker."[33] Hartmann, in turn, saw his neo-Kantian critic Hans Vaihinger "clinging to certain remnants of positive dogmatism."[34] On other occasions, he noticed a "relapse into the dogmatic narrow-mindedness of belief in an absolute knowledge," "a relapse into positive dogma," or a "falling back into dogmatic narrow-mindedness."[35] Hartmann feared that even Kant's philosophy contained "remnants of a naive dogmatic realism" or "a remnant of the old metaphysical dogmatism."[36] This imagery of remnants and relapses was also quite prominent in Vaihinger. Like so many, he interpreted the history of philosophy as a gradual triumph of criticism over dogmatism: "Day after day the dogmatic opponents recede, and more and more critique conquers the field." Against this background, Hartmann's pessimism appeared to him as a "last flare-up of idealistic dogmatism and a regrettable relapse into a mythological period which modern thought believed to have long since overcome." The implication was clear: "Hartmann's system is not for the future."[37]

* * *

What these polemics illustrate is that dogmatism had outspoken connotations of pastness. Not only did philosophers invoke the authority of Kant to accuse others of poor philosophizing, but they also interpreted traces of dogmatic thinking as remnants of a pre-Kantian past, which as such had no place in modern critical philosophy. In doing so, German philosophers resembled the history of science authors examined earlier in this chapter. Their view of Kant as marking a watershed in the history of philosophy was similar to Whewell-inspired narratives about Bacon inaugurating a new era in the history of science.[38] Also, the philosophers' habit of interpreting each and every trace of

---

[33] Gustav Knauer, *Das Facit aus E. v. Hartmann's Philosophie des Unbewussten* (Berlin: L. Heimann, 1873), 55. "Vain dogmatizing" might be an allusion to Glanvill's *The Vanity of Dogmatizing* (discussed in Chapter 2).

[34] Eduard von Hartmann, *Neukantianismus, Schopenhauerianismus und Hegelianismus in ihrer Stellung zu den philosophischen Aufgaben der Gegenwart* (Berlin: C. Duncker, 1877), 24.

[35] Ibid., 58, 79, 103; Eduard von Hartmann, *Philosophie des Unbewussten*, 5th ed. (Berlin: Carl Duncker, 1873), 826.

[36] Eduard von Hartmann, "Zur Orientirung in der Philosophie der letzten hundert Jahre" (1875), in Hartmann, *Gesammelte Studien und Aufsätze gemeinverständlichen Inhalts* (Berlin: Carl Duncker, 1876), 549–76, at 559; Hartmann, *Kritische Grundlegung des transcendentalen Realismus* (Berlin: Carl Duncker, 1875), 51.

[37] Hans Vaihinger, *Hartmann, Dühring und Lange: Zur Geschichte der deutschen Philosophie im XIX. Jahrhundert: Ein kritischer Essay* (Iserlohn: J. Baedeker, 1876), 202–3.

[38] As ibid., 31 put it: "Three things are necessary for the study of philosophy: First Kant, second Kant, third Kant!"

dogmatism in the present as a relapse or "setback" (*Rückschlag*) to the dark age of pre-Kantian philosophy was related to Whewell's belief that modern scientists ought to leave all dogmatism behind.[39] Because of their commitment to the progress of learning, most of them agreed that dogmatism, in the apt phrasing of a German orthopedist, had become an "anachronism."[40]

Clearly, then, scholars accusing each other of dogmatic thinking did more than challenge their opponents' claim to virtue: they were engaging in "temporal othering," by which we mean the deliberate exclusion of a person, school, or movement from the time that is called the "present." Charges of dogmatism were premised on the idea of a border between the present and the past, with most speakers positioning themselves on the modern side of the border while locating their "old-fashioned" opponents on the other side.[41] In the polemics featured in this chapter, such a "denial of coevalness" (to borrow a term from anthropologist Johannes Fabian) took on two basic forms.[42] In the mildest form, scholars argued that dogmatism was on its way to disappearing but had not yet completely vanished.[43] Without detracting from dogmatism's obsoleteness, this variant still allowed for a "contemporaneity of the non-contemporaneous." In a more radical version, however, the present had no room at all for superannuated modes of thinking. The metaphors of relapse and setback as used in the Pessimism Controversy were the most conspicuous expressions of such relentless othering in time: they relegated all dogmatism to a time before the modern age. As we shall see in later chapters, such strategies of othering would remain a feature of attacks on dogmatism, not only in an age of progress but also, more recently, in a time committed to "innovation."

---

[39] E. Dühring, *Kritische Geschichte der Philosophie von ihren Anfängen bis zur Gegenwart* (Berlin: L. Heimann, 1873), 235.

[40] G. Biedermeier, *Pragmatische und Begriffswissenschaftliche Geschichts-Schreibung der Philosophie* (Prague: F. Tempsky, 1870), 18.

[41] Such "politics of periodization" are the subject of Chris Lorenz and Berber Bevernage (eds.), *Breaking Up Time: Negotiating the Borders between Present, Past, and Future* (Göttingen: Vandenhoeck & Ruprecht, 2013).

[42] Johannes Fabian, *Time and the Other: How Anthropology Makes Its Object* (New York: Columbia University Press, 1983), 25–35.

[43] For example, Eduard von Hartmann, "Anfange naturwissenschaftlicher Selbsterkenntnis" (1875), in Hartmann, *Gesammelte Studien*, 445–59, at 448. See also, a little later, Theodor Beer, *Die Weltanschauung eines modernen Naturforschers: Ein nichtkritisches Referat über Mach's "Analyse der Empfindungen"* (Dresden: Carl Reissner, 1903), 13.

4

As Infallible as the Pope

Demarcating Science and Religion

On a Sunday afternoon in November 1876, one of the more remarkable figures on the London speaking circuit, Gustavus George Zerffi, addressed the Sunday Lecture Society on the theme of "Science and Dogma." Zerffi was a former Hungarian journalist and secret service spy who had turned into a Victorian art historian and science popularizer.[1] A frequent speaker at the Sunday Lecture Society, he used the occasion to explain that the modern age had no room for archaic habits like dogmatic reasoning. From an evolutionary point of view, dogmatism had belonged to primitive societies. It had been able to maintain its reign in the dark Middle Ages, when scholastic theologians had sold "inherited prejudices and musty incredibilities" as divinely sanctioned knowledge. Fortunately, however, the rise of modern science had abandoned these "idolatries and dogmatic monstrosities" by cultivating rational and independent thinking. In principle, therefore, the age of science that was the nineteenth century should be free from "narrow-minded dogmatism." In fact, however, controversies of the kind provoked by Charles Darwin's *On the Origins of Species* (1859) and the biblical criticism pursued in John William Parker's *Essays and Reviews* (1860) showed that dogmatism still held sway over the minds of the Christian clergy in particular. By condemning the latest advances in biology, geology, or biblical studies as threats to

---

[1] Tibor Frank, *Ein Diener seiner Herren: Werdegang des österreichischen Geheimagenten Gustav Zerffi (1820–1892)*, trans. Péter Mádl and Piroska Draskóczy (Vienna: Böhlau, 2002).

Christian orthodoxy, ecclesiastical authorities like Archibald Campbell Tait, the Archbishop of Canterbury, behaved as if "the wheel of time had been stopped, or even was to be turned backwards."[2]

In mid-Victorian England, such anticlerical voices could be heard widely, both in the Sunday Lecture Society and in broader circles of "scientific naturalists"—a loose label for scientists and science popularizers who paired rationalist leanings with progressive and anti-religious stances.[3] John Tyndall, for instance, seldom let an opportunity pass to distance himself from the "dogmatism, fanaticism, and intolerance" that he saw epitomized in the Roman Catholic Church.[4] Thomas Henry Huxley, likewise, made short shrift with religious orthodoxies that treated the book of Genesis as an alternative to *The Origins of Species*: "History records that whenever science and dogmatism have been fairly opposed, the latter has been forced to retire from the lists, bleeding and crushing, if not annihilated; scotched if not slain."[5] The X Club, to which both Huxley and Tyndall belonged, even defined itself as anti-dogmatic. Its members, said Thomas Archer Hirst, were united by "devotion to science, pure and free, untrammelled by religious dogmas."[6]

Although these polemics offer further evidence of what Chapter 3 called the archaic connotations of dogmatism in an age of progress, the science and religion debates to which Zerffi, Tyndall, and Huxley contributed also left another imprint on the term. Not only did dogmatism serve as a rhetorical weapon for contending parties in debates over Darwinism, scientific progress, and materialist thinking, but these debates in turn also gave a new twist to an old term. On a much wider scale than in eighteenth-century France (Chapter 2), dogmatism came to be associated with faithful allegiance to a religious creed or blind obedience to a supreme pontiff. Interestingly, this frame was adopted not only by scientific naturalists but also, no less frequently, by Christian critics

[2] G. G. Zerffi, *Dogma and Science: A Lecture Delivered before the Sunday Lecture Society . . .* (London: Sunday Lecture Society, [1876]), 3, 4, 18, 3, in response to Archibald Campbell [Tait], *Some Thoughts on the Duties of the Established Church of England as a National Church: Being Seven Addresses Delivered at His Second Visitation* (London: Macmillan and Co., 1876).

[3] Ruth Barton, "Sunday Lecture Societies: Naturalistic Scientists, Unitarians, and Secularists Unite against Sabbatarian Legislation," in Gowan Dawson and Bernard Lightman (eds.), *Victorian Scientific Naturalism: Community, Identity, Continuity* (Chicago: University of Chicago Press, 2014), 189–219. On the term "scientific naturalism," see Gowan Dawson and Bernard Lightman, "Introduction," ibid., 1–24, esp. 3–10.

[4] John Tyndall, *Address Delivered Before the British Association Assembled at Belfast with Additions* (London: Longmans, Green, and Co., 1874), 62.

[5] [Thomas Henry Huxley], "Darwin on the Origin of Species," *The Westminster Review* 17 (1860): 541–70, at 556.

[6] Quoted in Ruth Barton, *The X Club: Power and Authority in Victorian Science* (Chicago: University of Chicago Press, 2018), 13.

of militant Darwinists like Huxley. "Dogmatism," in other words, became a shorthand term for pretensions of infallibility, be it in the church or in science.

*   *   *

Where did Zerffi's idea of an unresolvable conflict between science and dogmatism come from? A perhaps obvious source was the emerging genre of "warfare" books like John William Draper's *History of the Conflict Between Religion and Science* (1874) and Andrew Dickson White's *The Warfare of Science* (1876). Drawing on a long tradition of Protestant polemicizing against the supposed irrationalism and authoritarianism of the Roman Catholic Church, these two widely read titles set the tone for many others by emplotting the history of science as a permanent battle between scientific curiosity and ecclesiastical oppression. Although Draper and White were not against religion as such, they argued on the basis of historical examples that narrow-minded theology had always done much harm to science, especially in the hands of church authorities. Accordingly, Draper and White believed that both science and religion would benefit from shaking off the yoke of dogmatic theology.[7]

In addition, the Victorian periodical press offered plenty of opportunities for men like Zerffi to familiarize themselves with the idea that science and dogma were antagonistic. They only needed to pick up a copy of *The Fortnightly Review*, a leading progressive periodical, to stumble upon Francis Galton's argument that "the blighting effect of dogmatism upon scientific investigation is shown both in Catholic and Protestant countries" or to encounter Ernest Renan's view that science and dogma were "incompatible."[8] Also, in the same review, an article on "The Clergy in Relation to Modern Dogmatism and Modern Thought" told its readers that the English intellectual landscape was divided between freethinkers and "dogmatists," also known as "lovers of ancient stereotyped opinion," who did not know better than to tell their flock: "Hold fast; close your ears to the vicious science of these degenerate days; walk in the old paths; be rigid, and you will be right."[9]

What reinforced this juxtaposition of science and dogma was that some of the clergy ridiculed in *The Fortnightly Review* claimed the adjective "dogmatic" for their own purposes. They did so, among other things, in

---

[7] James C. Ungureanu, *Science, Religion, and the Protestant Tradition: Retracing the Origins of Conflict* (Pittsburgh: University of Pittsburgh Press, 2019).

[8] Francis Galton, "On the Causes which Operate to Create Scientific Men," *The Fortnightly Review* 19 (1873): 345–51, at 348; [George Henry Lewis], "Causeries," *The Fortnightly Review* 5 (1866): 241–6, at 242.

[9] G. R. Wynne, "The Clergy in Relation to Modern Dogmatism and Modern Thought," *The Fortnightly Review* 4 (1866): 513–32, at 514.

response to a liberal Protestant penchant for "unsectarian" or "undogmatic" forms of Christianity, with which conservative clergy deemed it impossible to win the battle against modern heresies like those espoused in *Essays and Reviews*.[10] An "undogmatic church," wrote canon Frederick Oakeley in 1866, "can be no bulwark against infidelity."[11] In a similar vein, Richard F. Littledale argued "that a nominal, undogmatic Church" is unable to satisfy the hunger of the human soul.[12] An Anglican vicar concluded from this that his church should not be afraid of dogmatic teaching. "The fact is, a Church is a communion: there must be terms of communion; and those terms must be dogmas."[13] Interestingly, it was these ecclesiastical polemics that prompted Matthew Arnold, the English poet and cultural critic, to write his *Literature and Dogma* (1873), a Victorian bestseller that was one long attack on the "pseudo-science of Church dogma."[14] Critics of the church, in other words, borrowed their rhetorical weapons from quarreling parties within the church, just as happened the other way around.

The Vatican Council (1869–70) also contributed to this effect, not only by proclaiming the dogma of papal infallibility but also by defining "dogmas" as doctrinal formulas binding for all Catholic believers—a much stricter definition than any theologian before had dared to propose.[15] In Britain just as elsewhere, Protestants responded with dismay to this perceived assault on the freedom of thought (which they liked to think of as a fruit of the Protestant Reformation). In an age when science and religion already seemed to part ways, there was no more telling illustration of the anti-scientific attitude common among ecclesiastical authorities than the dogmatism of the red-robed cardinals gathered in Saint Peter's Basilica.[16] In his *History*

---

[10] Josef L. Altholz, "The Mind of Victorian Orthodoxy: Anglican Responses to 'Essays and Reviews,' 1860–1864," *Church History* 51, no. 2 (1982): 186–97; Victoria Shea and William Whitla, "Reading 'An Epoch in the History of Opinion,'" in Victoria Shea and William Whitla (eds.), *Essays and Reviews: The 1860 Text and Its Reading* (Charlottesville: University Press of Virginia, 2000), 1–130, esp. 28–46.

[11] Frederick Oakeley, *The Leading Topics of Dr. Pusey's Recent Work* . . . (London: Longmans, Green, and Co., 1866), 8–9 (page headers).

[12] Richard F. Littledale, *The Crisis of Disestablishment: A Lecture Delivered at the Mechanics' Institute, Bradford, May 16th, 1870* (London: G. J. Palmer, 1870), 6.

[13] Archibald Weir, "Dogma," in Archibald Weir and William Dalrymple MacLagan (eds.), *The Church and the Age: Essays on the Principles and Present Position of the Anglican Church*, vol. 2 (London: John Murray, 1872), 297–326, at 319.

[14] Matthew Arnold, *Literature and Dogma: An Essay Towards a Better Apprehension of the Bible* (London: Smith, Elder, & Co., 1873), 379.

[15] Hubert Filser, *Dogma, Dogmen, Dogmatik: Eine Untersuchung zur Begründung und zur Entstehungsgeschichte einer theologischen Disziplin von der Reformation bis zur Spätaufklärung* (Munster: LIT, 2001), 707–8.

[16] Robert Fitzsimons, "The Church of England and the First Vatican Council," *The Journal of Religious History* 27, no. 1 (2003): 29–46; Geoffrey Scarre, "Fallible Infallibility? Gladstone's Anti-

of the Conflict Between Religion and Science, a clearly outraged Draper discussed the Council at great length, quoting extensively from its reports to prove that the Roman Catholic Church was intent on opposing all science, all free inquiry, and all honest searching for truth. Dogma had become a matter of "blind faith" or obedience to an authority that was unable to justify its rule by arguments other than a claim to infallibility.[17] As we shall see, this connection between dogmatism and infallibility would be picked up by many a Victorian man of science.

In short, when Zerffi and others leached out against a dogmatism that "burns incense to stupefy our senses, light candles to obscure our sight, revives the postures and ceremonies of past ages, commits anachronisms in science and art, and amuses the masses with old and obsolete buffooneries to prevent them from thinking,"[18] they could draw not only on an emerging genre of "warfare" books like Draper's and White's but also, more broadly, on a sense of antagonism between scientific and dogmatic thinking that was common currency among Darwinists and anti-Darwinists alike.

* * *

If the wide prevalence of "dogmatism" in Victorian intellectual discourse helps explain why Christian critics of Darwinism were routinely being accused of "ecclesiastical dogmatism,"[19] it also makes it understandable why those critics could turn the tables, as Bernard Lightman puts it, by blaming scientific naturalists of a dogmatism no less rigid than that of the pope.[20] They returned the compliment, in other words, by observing that "the stiff dogmatism of a stagnant orthodoxy" was being substituted by "a more dangerous dogmatism of scepticism, and infidelity, which threatens to sweep away, Bible, Church, orthodoxy, and all for which it is worth living."[21]

Vatican Pamphlets in the Light of Mill's *On Liberty*," *Victorian Literature and Culture* 44, no. 2 (2016): 223–37.

[17] John William Draper, *History of the Conflict Between Religion and Science* (New York: D. Appleton and Company, 1874), 362, 365.

[18] G. G. Zerffi, *The Origin and the Abstract and Concrete Nature of the Devil: A Lecture Delivered before the Sunday Lecture Society . . .* (London: Thomas Scott, 1874), 28.

[19] T. H. Huxley, "Agnosticism and Christianity," *The Nineteenth Century* 25 (1889): 937–64, at 945.

[20] Bernard Lightman, "The Creed of Science and Its Critics," in Martin Hewitt (ed.), *The Victorian World* (London: Routledge, 2012), 449–65, at 450.

[21] John Muehleisen-Arnold, *English Biblical Criticism, and the Pentateuch, from a German Point of View*, vol. 1 (London: Longman, Green, Longman, Roberts & Green, 1864), 13. Cf. Samuel Wainwright, *Christian Certainty* (London: Hatchard and Co., 1865), 94; Wainwright, *Scientific Sophisms: A Review of Current Theories Concerning Atoms, Apes, and Men* (London: Hodder and Stoughton, 1881), 3.

Such charges of scientific dogmatism gained traction not only among pastors and theologians but also among Christian scientists like those gathered in the Victoria Institute, a learned society founded in 1865 with the aim of defending "the great truths revealed in Holy Scripture" against "the opposition of science, falsely so called."[22] Already in the first meeting, the institute's vice president declared: "Whatever we may say in favour of theological dogmas, we cannot permit dogmatism in the world of science."[23] Papers read at subsequent meetings left no doubt as to who these "scientific dogmatizers" were. The phrase referred to "the Haeckels, the Spencers, and the Huxleys of the present day," who preached "the new dogma of Evolution by natural selection" to convert people to a "scientific faith" incompatible with the Christian belief that God created and sustains the world.[24]

This charge of scientific dogmatism proceeded from two assumptions. The first is that scientific naturalists were eager to turn scientific hypotheses into quasi-infallible certainties. As Samuel Rowles Pattison asked rhetorically in an 1875 address on geological timescales: "Why then, with all this geological evidence of uncertainty recorded by the masters of science, do the same masters or their disciples, dogmatize on the subject of long periods? Why has this scientific dogmatism crept into elementary treatises, and is there laid down with all the confidence of axiomatic knowledge?"[25] Other Victoria Institute lecturers likewise spoke about dogmatism when they saw unproven hypotheses being presented as well-ascertained facts,[26] thereby illustrating that staunch empiricism was attractive for scholars in search of scientific arguments against the "new materialism" of Darwin's disciples.[27] Second, just as "dogmatic ecclesiasticism" was understood to amount to believing on authority, scientific dogmatism was equated with "a faith which relies on

---

[22] Stuart Mathieson, *Evangelicals and the Philosophy of Science: The Victoria Institute, 1865–1939* (London: Routledge, 2021), 32.

[23] "First Ordinary Meeting, June 4, 1866," *Journal of the Transactions of the Victoria Institute* 1 (1867): 84–114, at 113.

[24] Joseph Hassell, "Evolution by Natural Selection Tested by Its Own Canon, and Shown to Be Untenable," *Journal of the Transactions of the Victoria Institute* 19 (1885): 53–67, at 55, 65.

[25] S. R. Pattison, "On the Chronology of Recent Geology," *Journal of the Transactions of the Victoria Institute* 10 (1877): 1–26, at 25.

[26] J. M'Cann, "Force and Its Manifestations," *Journal of the Transactions of the Victoria Institute* 7 (1874): 96–123, at 113; J. E. Howard, "Influence of True and False Philosophy on the Formation of Character," *Journal of the Transactions of the Victoria Institute* 12 (1879): 164–84, at 170.

[27] Lionel S. Beale, "Dictatorial Scientific Utterances and the Decline of Thought," *Journal of the Transactions of the Victoria Institute* 16 (1883): 201–27, at 208; Beale, "On the New Materialism," ibid., 238–45.

authority."[28] As John Elliot Howard exclaimed in a response to Tyndall's much-debated Belfast address of 1874: "This is neither the old chemistry nor the new chemistry, nor science in any shape; but simple and pure assertion—DOGMA, to be received and held on the authority of Tyndall alone!"[29]

Conservative Christians were not the only ones who worried about evolutionary thinking taking on dogmatic forms. Figures as diverse as Samuel Butler, William Graham, William Samuel Lilly, and Lewis Wright warned in print against a "new dogmatism" or "dogmatism of science" that they feared would be no less ruthless than "the tyranny of dogmatic creeds" had been in times past.[30] Huxley in particular was seen by many as a prophet of "dogmatic atheism" because of his never-ceasing fight against the church and his advocacy of an alternative worldview known as "agnosticism."[31] Along these lines, William Sanday, writing in *The Contemporary Review*, depicted Huxley as a truly dogmatic theologian, "repaying to theology the same sort of measure which . . . theology dealt out to him."[32] Even in the pages of *Nature*, Huxley was said to be "fanatical" and driven by a "dogmatism" of which Darwin, more cautious than some of his disciples, would certainly have disapproved.[33]

* * *

What these examples show is that dogmatism was not regarded as a prerogative of Christian theologians. Scientific naturalists, too, found themselves being diagnosed with dogmatism. Interestingly, however, the language in which such charges were made continued to be religious or became even more so in relation to the Vatican Council. Even before the council had adjourned, critics began to speak about "Pope Huxley" and his habit of adopting "the tone of

---

[28] N. Whitley, "The Palaeolithic Age Examined," *Journal of the Transactions of the Victoria Institute* 8 (1875): 4–23, at 4–5.

[29] John Elliot Howard, "An Examination of the Belfast Address of the British Association, 1874, from a Scientific Point of View," *Journal of the Transactions of the Victoria Institute* 10 (1877): 104–29, at 122.

[30] Samuel Butler, *Life and Habit* (London: Trübner & Co., 1878), 40; William Graham, *The Creed of Science: Religious, Moral, and Social* (London: C. Kegan Paul & Co., 1881), 237, 196; Lewis Wright, "The New Dogmatism," *The Contemporary Review* 54 (1888): 192–213; William Samuel Lilly, *On Shibboleths* (London: Chapman and Hall, 1892), 13. See also, at the other side of the Atlantic, George M. Gould, "The Dogmatism of Science," *Science* 2, no. 43 (1895): 554–5.

[31] [Richard Holt Hutton], "The Approach of Dogmatic Atheism," *The Spectator* 47 (1874): 1525–7; Unus de Multis [pseudonym of William Allingham], "Modern Prophets," *Fraser's Magazine* 16 (1877): 273–92.

[32] W. Sanday, "Professor Huxley as a Theologian," *The Contemporary Review* 62 (1892): 336–52, at 352.

[33] Argyll, "The Struggle of Parts in the Organism," *Nature* 25, no. 627 (1881): 6–7, at 7.

a Papal bull,—containing violent censures—almost excommunications *latae sententiae*,—as well as dogmatic decrees."[34] Within years, such comparisons between dogmatic scientists and infallible popes achieved commonplace status. When Huxley, writing in 1871, distinguished between "Scientific Authority, as represented by Reason and Fact" and "Infallible Authority, as represented by the Holy Father and the Catholic Church," the upshot of his argument was that Darwin's critics were hopelessly confusing the one with the other.[35] Samuel Butler wrote that the "men of science now most prominent" reminded him of "the Roman priesthood."[36] Others warned against "the utterance of assertions as arrogant in theoretical science, as papal dogmatism is in theological belief."[37] An 1871 article challenged Alfred Russell Wallace's "angry dogmatism" on the ground that not even Wallace, a leading evolutionary thinker, could lay claim to "Infallibility."[38] In a more resigned mood, Oxford professor Edward Bouverie Pusey was being told by a colleague: "We have no right to complain of dogmatism, for the scientific men of the day surpass the theologians in this."[39] Likewise, a British engineer drew the papal analogy in commenting on the authoritative stance taken by some high-profile naturalists: "Scientific Popes are no more infallible than theological ones, and both scientific as well as theological popery have risen into power very similarly."[40] Clearly, anticlerical associations as originally developed by Voltaire and Rousseau were rising to considerable prominence.

To the extent that this was a response to Vatican church politics around 1870, one might expect that its impact was short-lived. In reality, however, "dogmatic infallibility" became a rhetorical commonplace that proved to be applicable in contexts and periods beyond the Darwinian controversies. Book reviewers in *Nature* complained repeatedly about dogmatic infallibility ("a vein of dogmatic infallibility is particularly apparent in dealing with geological problems") or "infallible dogma."[41] Arguments along the line that "speculations in science are never intended to be infallible dogmas" drew on the same

---

[34] [Richard Holt Hutton], "Pope Huxley," *The Spectator* 43 (1870): 135–6, at 136.

[35] T. H. Huxley, "Mr. Darwin's Critics," *The Contemporary Review* 18 (1871): 443–76, at 456.

[36] Samuel Butler to May Butler, May 3, 1880, in *The Correspondence of Samuel Butler with His Sister May*, ed. Daniel F. Howard (Berkeley: University of California Press, 1962), 83–5, at 85.

[37] [Henry Cole], *Fifty Years of Public Work of Sir Henry Cole . . .*, ed. Alan S. and Henriette Cole, vol. 1 (London: George Bell, 1884), 187.

[38] H. Howorth, "A New View of Darwinism," *Nature* 4, no. 89 (1871): 200–1, at 201.

[39] Quoted in Henry Parry Liddon, *Life of Edward Bouverie Pusey*, vol. 4 (London: Longmans, Green, and Co., 1897), 335.

[40] S. Alfred Varley, "Is Science Disciplined Knowledge, or Is It Something Else?" *The Telegraphical Journal and Electrical Review* 28 (1891): 4–6, 44–8, 96, at 45.

[41] J. S. G., "The Fenland," *Nature* 18, no. 463 (1878): 514–16, at 514; [William Johnson Sollas], "Geologies and Deluges," *Nature* 50, no. 1299 (1894): 505–10, at 506.

commonplace.[42] Although we should add that "dogmatic" continued to be used synonymously with ill-founded or unprovable, the science and religion debate of the 1870s expanded the term's range of connotations: "infallible rules" and "infallible dicta" had become part of it.[43]

* * *

To illustrate that British scientists were not alone responsible for this, we end this chapter on a comparative note, with a brief glance at a German equivalent of the British debate. Just as Huxley was perceived both as a warrior against "ecclesiastical dogmatism" and as an epitome of "scientific dogmatism," so the German zoologist Ernst Haeckel—a good friend of Huxley—earned a reputation for pope-like dogmatism because of the zeal with which he promoted Darwinian biology as an alternative to revealed religion. Notably, in the debates surrounding him in the late 1870s, the ties between dogmatism and obedience to infallible authorities were knotted as firmly as on the other side of the Channel.

Haeckel's own aversion to dogmatism became apparent in a public exchange with his former teacher Rudolf Virchow.[44] In 1877, Virchow had created a stir at the annual conference of the German Association of Naturalists and Physicians by arguing that evolutionary theory should not be taught in secondary schools as long as it was a mere hypothesis. In an empiricist mode reminiscent of the Victoria Institute, he had warned that people would lose their trust in science if schoolbooks confronted children with "edifices of mere theory and speculation." "Nowhere," Virchow had added, "is the necessity of such a limitation more conspicuous, than in the very province of the doctrine of generation," given that some scientists tried to turn it into a "religion of evolution," aspiring to take the place formerly reserved for church dogma.[45] As Haeckel took these words as directed at himself, he replied in print, stating sarcastically that the clerical press has reason to rejoice about a former "opponent of dogma" now defending ecclesiastical dogma against Darwinian biology. Apparently, "Virchow now finds the only sure basis for instruction in the dogmas of the church." Virchow-style school teaching would take "the

---

[42] "The Nature of Scientific Hypotheses," *The Mendel Journal* 1 (1909): 199–203, at 200.

[43] N. N., "Odium Medicum," *Nature* 37, no. 952 (1888): 289–90, at 290; N. N., "The British Association," *Nature* 44, no. 1138 (1891): 371–8, at 384.

[44] On which, see Robert J. Richards, *The Tragic Sense of Life: Ernst Haeckel and the Struggle over Evolutionary Thought* (Chicago: University of Chicago Press, 2008), 318–41.

[45] Rudolf Virchow, *Die Freiheit der Wissenschaft im modernen Staat* . . . (Berlin: Wiegandt, Hempel & Parey, 1877), 22, 18, 29. The English translation is taken from Rudolf Virchow, *The Freedom of Science in the Modern State* . . . (London: John Murray, 1878), 41, 32–3, 57.

dogma of the resurrection of the body as a basis of medicine [and] the dogma of infallibility as a basis for psychology . . . dogmas which not only are not proved by any facts whatever, but on the contrary, stand in the most trenchant contradiction to the most obvious facts of natural experience and fly in the face of all human reason."[46] Haeckel knew, of course, that Virchow had not returned to the fold of the church—his aversion to ecclesiastical dogmatism was unabated—but apparently believed that the association with church dogma sufficed to discredit his former teacher's reservations regarding the school teaching of evolution theory.[47]

If Haeckel referred to the dogma of infallibility, so did many a commentator on the Virchow–Haeckel exchange. Carl Vogt, the German-Swiss zoologist who on an earlier occasion had been accused by Virchow of ecclesiastical dogmatism,[48] depicted his quarreling colleagues as "pope" and "anti-pope." "The sense of their own infallibility, which is the very note of the papal office, is specially prominent, and determines the whole tenor of their thoughts."[49] While authors siding with Haeckel often emphasized Virchow's loyalty to church authority, for instance by calling him a "papists' servant" (Pfaffenknecht),[50] the trope of infallibility was used most frequently by critics of Haeckel. The Würzburg anatomist Carl Semper, though sympathizing with Darwin, censured Haeckel's "infallible condemnatory formulas" as well as his habitual use of adverbs like "surely," "undoubtedly," and "evidently," which Semper interpreted as evidence of Haeckel's "faith in his own infallibility."[51] "'Haeckel locutus est' is being thundered from Jena [where Haeckel taught];

---

[46] Ernst Haeckel, *Freie Wissenschaft und freie Lehre: Eine Entgegnung auf Rudolf Virchow's Münchener Rede über "Die Freiheit der Wissenschaft im modernen Staat"* (Stuttgart: E. Schweizerbart, 1878), 64, 65, 66. The English translation is taken from Ernst Haeckel, *Freedom in Science and Teaching* (New York: D. Appleton and Company, 1879), 80, 81, 82.

[47] On underlying issues regarding the professionalization of German biology at the time, see Andreas Daum, *Wissenschaftspopularisierung im 19. Jahrhundert: Bürgerliche Kultur, naturwissenschaftliche Bildung und die deutsche Öffentlichkeit 1848–1914*, 2nd ed. (Munich: Oldenbourg, 2002), 66–71.

[48] Rudolf Virchow, "Die Einheits-Bestrebungen in der wissenschaftlichen Medicin," in Virchow, *Gesammelte Abhandlungen zur wissenschaftlichen Medicin* (Frankfurt am Main: Meidinger Sohn & Comp., 1856), 1–56, at 18.

[49] Carl Vogt, "Papst und Gegenpapst," *Neue Freie Presse* (September 21, 1878), quoted in Gustav Miller's English translation, "Pope and Anti-Pope," *The Popular Science Monthly* 14, no. 3 (1879): 320–5, at 320.

[50] Quoted in N. N., "Gloria in excelsis Deo etc.," *Augsburger Sonntagsblatt* 37, nos. 51–2 (1877): 403–7, 409–11, at 410. For a more nuanced defense against Virchow's charge of dogmatism, see Otto Caspari, *Virchow und Haeckel vor dem Forum der methodologischen Forschung* (Augsburg: Lampert & Comp., 1878), esp. 32.

[51] Carl Semper, *Offener Brief an Herrn Prof. Haeckel in Jena* (Hamburg: W. Mauke & Sohne, 1877), 8 and *Der Haeckelismus in der Zoologie* (Hamburg: W. Mauke & Sohne, 1876), 28.

hence all of us must keep quiet."[52] A former student of Virchow, likewise, saw Haeckel as sitting "on a throne of infallibility," issuing "dogmas of an infallible science."[53] Although the impact of these polemics was probably not too large,[54] they illustrate that, in Germany just as in England, dogmatism was linked firmly to infallibility as exercised by the pope.[55]

In sum, whereas dogmatism before the 1870s was mostly associated with ill-founded statements and unprovable assumptions, the post-Darwinian controversies brought another connotation to the fore: dogmatism was equated with claims to infallibility and obedience to authority. Dogmatism became, in Huxley's words, a matter of "blind acceptance of authority" or bowing to "the Baal of authority."[56] In the idiom of a later generation (Chapter 7), we might say that late nineteenth-century scientists in their attempts at demarcating science and religion cemented a link between dogmatism and authoritarianism that was going to last throughout much of the twentieth century.

---

[52] Semper, *Offener Brief*, 4–5.

[53] J. A. Sch[?], "Ein moderner Unfehlbarer," *Hessische Blätter* (July 3, 6, 13, 17, 1878): unpag. This article originally appeared in the conservative newspaper *Germania*.

[54] Richards, *Tragic Sense of Life*, 300 n. 67.

[55] See also, in a similar vein, Houston Stewart Chamberlain, "Büchners Sturz," *Die Neue Rundschau* 6, no. 1 (1895): 572–84, at 578; Th. G. Masaryk, *Die philosophischen und sociologischen Grundlagen des Marxismus: Studien zur socialen Frage* (Vienna: Carl Konegen, 1899), 63.

[56] Huxley, "Mr. Darwin's Critics," 458.

5

The Prince of Dogmatists

Stereotypical Attributions

It is a matter of dispute what Montaigne meant when he dubbed Aristotle "the prince of Dogmatists."[1] In sixteenth-century France, "dogmatism" was not yet the pejorative term that it would later become. As we saw in Chapter 2, Montaigne used it primarily as a descriptive label for a distinct school of ancient philosophy. What is puzzling, however, is that Montaigne did not attribute to Aristotle the usual marks of this dogmatic school, such as a straightforward teaching of well-ascertained truths. Instead, he highlighted the density of Aristotle's language, the impenetrability of his thought, and a searching attitude that seemed to put Aristotle closer to skepticism than to dogmatism ("It is in fact a form of Pyrrhonism under a form of decision").[2] Did Montaigne perhaps intend to say that Aristotle, rather than himself being a first-class dogmatist, served as the highest authority for dogmatists like that anonymous philosopher from Pisa of whom Montaigne had said earlier that he was "such an Aristotelian" that he considered "conformity to the teachings of Aristotle" as "the touchstone and canon of all truth"?[3] This reading would be in line with another of Montaigne's ironic compliments, namely that Aristotle served as "the god of scholastic science," whose teachings were taught "as

---

[1] See, for example, François Rigolot, "Montaigne et Aristote: la conversion à l'*Ethique à Nicomaque*," in Ullrich Langer (ed.), *Au-delà de la poétique: Aristote et la littérature de la Renaissance* (Geneva: Droz, 2002), 47–63; David Lewis Schaefer, *The Political Philosophy of Montaigne* (Ithaca: Cornell University Press, 1990), 84–6.

[2] Montaigne, *Essays*, trans. George B. Ives and Grace Norton, vol. 2 (Cambridge, MA: Harvard University Press, 1925), 273.

[3] Montaigne, *Essays*, trans. George B. Ives and Grace Norton, vol. 1 (Cambridge, MA: Harvard University Press, 1925), 203.

supreme law" and treated as just as indisputable as Lycurgus' law in Sparta.[4]

Whatever its intended meaning in Montaigne, "the prince of Dogmatists" became a tag that nineteenth-century authors eagerly used in criticizing dogmatists of various shapes and stripes. The phrase was applied to Galen, Paracelsus, Augustine, John Calvin, and René Descartes, among others, with all the pejorative meanings that dogmatism had meanwhile acquired.[5] Clearly, in these nineteenth-century texts, "prince of dogmatists" conveyed that the named figures *themselves* had been excessively dogmatic (with Augustine, for instance, appearing as "the [most] vicious one of all dogmatists").[6] As such, they resembled other historical figures with an established reputation for dogmatic reasoning. The nineteenth-century resurgence of interest in the work of Thomas Hobbes, for instance, was accompanied by a spirited debate on his allegedly dogmatic character traits as well as the dogmatic nature of his theory of sovereignty.[7] Hobbes' dogmatism even came to serve as a yardstick for measuring others. Mid-century critics of Auguste Comte, for instance, called him "unrivalled" in his dogmatism, "with perhaps the single exception of Hobbes," and "as dogmatic as Hobbes, or, if possible, more so."[8]

If historical figures could have such reputations for dogmatism, it is worth inquiring whether nineteenth-century or early twentieth-century scholars found figureheads of dogmatism also among their contemporaries. To what extent was dogmatism seen as embodied, not only by scholars in times past (Chapter 3) or by a church that was supposedly in conflict with science (Chapter 4) but also by present-day "princes of dogmatism"? And if individuals could be turned into negative models, held up as warning examples in classes

---

[4] Montaigne, *Essays*, vol. 2, 318.

[5] Franklin Chase Clark, "A Contribution to the Study of Medicine," *Detroit Medical Journal* 1 (1877): 721–37, at 725; J. B. Heard, *Alexandrian and Carthaginian Theology Contrasted: The Hulsean Lectures, 1892–93* (Edinburgh: T. & T. Clark, 1893), 47; Geo. W. Pickerill, "Cui Bono?" *The Medical Eclectic* 3 (1876): 174–83, at 178; [Thomas Wright], *The True Plan of a Living Temple; or, Man Considered in His Proper Relation to the Ordinary Occupations and Pursuits of Life*, vol. 3 (Edinburgh: Oliver & Boyd, 1830), 359; Francis Bowen, *Modern Philosophy: From Descartes to Schopenhauer and Hartmann* (New York: Scribner, Armstrong & Company, 1877), 23.

[6] Heard, *Alexandrian and Carthaginian Theology*, 47.

[7] James Mackintosh, *Dissertation on the Progress of Ethical Philosophy, Chiefly During the Seventeenth and Eighteenth Centuries* (Edinburgh: Adam and Charles Black, 1836 [1830]), 118–9 ("the most imperious and morose of dogmatists"); [James Mill], *A Fragment on Mackintosh: Being Strictures on Some Passages in the Dissertation by Sir James Mackintosh, Prefixed to the Encyclopaedia Britannica* (London: Baldwin and Cradock, 1835), 32–4; Frederick Denison Maurice, *Modern Philosophy, or a Treatise of Moral and Metaphysical Philosophy from the Fourteenth Century to the French Revolution, with a Glimpse into the Nineteenth Century* (London: Griffin, Bohn and Company, 1862), 410.

[8] N. N., review of *The Positive Philosophy of Auguste Comte* by Harriet Martineau, *The North American Review* 79 (1854): 200–29, at 207; "Mr. Mill on the Philosophy of Comte," *The Saturday Review* 19 (1865): 431–3, at 432.

and textbooks alike, could dogmatism also be linked to national or anti-Semitic stereotypes, thereby creating dangerous images of human collectives with a penchant for dogmatic thinking? This chapter will explore these questions by examining three kinds of stereotypes: (1) individual stereotypes of scholars whose names became bywords for dogmatism, (2) national stereotypes like the trope of "German dogmatism" as used by French scholars in the First World War, and (3) the anti-Semitic stereotype of "Jewish dogmatism" as propagated by the German physicist Johannes Stark prior to and during the Second World War.

*   *   *

How remarkable was it for nineteenth-century scholars to speak about "Hegelian dogmatism" or to argue that "the climax of dogmatism" had been reached by Hippolyte Taine?[9] As existing scholarship has shown, it was not uncommon to name virtues and vices after high-profile colleagues. German historians in the 1840s, for instance, spoke about "Rankean objectivity" to specify what they understood the abstract virtue of objectivity to look like in practice ("objectivity as practiced by Leopold von Ranke").[10] Some decades later, the English historian Edward Augustus Freeman did something similar in criticizing his colleague James Anthony Froude. He not only found Froude guilty of numerous inaccuracies but in the heat of controversy also went so far as to present his opponent as a paradigmatic example of the vice of inaccuracy. Like "Rankean objectivity," "Froude's disease" quickly became a proverbial phrase. It even found its way into student manuals, with the effect of Froude's name becoming a byword for a vice that all seriously intended historians tried to avoid.[11]

To what extent did something similar happen with dogmatism? At first sight, there seem to have been plenty of nineteenth-century scholars whose names evoked the specter of dogmatism. Ludwig Büchner, for instance, the Tübingen physiologist whose *Power and Matter* (1855) unleashed the so-called

---

[9] Otto Pfleiderer, *The Development in Theology in Germany since Kant and Its Progress in Great Britain since 1825*, trans. J. Frederick Smith (London: Swan Sonnenschein & Co., 1890), 133; [Henry James], "Taine's Italy," *The Nation* 6 (1868): 373–5, at 374.

[10] Herman Paul, "Ranke vs Schlosser: Pairs of Personae in Nineteenth-Century German Historiography," in Herman Paul (ed.), *How to Be a Historian: Scholarly Personae in Historical Studies, 1800–2000* (Manchester: Manchester University Press, 2019), 36–52.

[11] Ian Hesketh, "Diagnosing Froude's Disease: Boundary Work and the Discipline of History in Late-Victorian Britain," *History and Theory* 47, no. 3 (2008): 373–95; Ch.-V. Langlois and C. Seignobos, *Introduction aux études historiques* (Paris: Hachette et Cie., 1898), 101–2.

Materialism Controversy,[12] was widely known as a dogmatic defender of the view that everything in the world, ideas and sensations included, is reducible to matter. "A more dogmatic work" than *Power and Matter*, said the philosopher and theosophist Edward Douglas Fawcett, "we may search in vain among the Patristic literature to find."[13] (Note that in this comment not Hobbes but early Christian theologians served as a standard of comparison.) Drawing on Montaigne's sneer at Aristotle, Karl Pearson even called Büchner "the prince of dogmatists," because of his staunch defense of a position that Pearson found hopelessly indefensible.[14]

Importantly, however, Büchner did not earn this epithet because of a dispositional inclination toward dogmatic thinking but because the materialist system that he laid out in his book was as grandiose as it was rigid and inhospitable to criticism. Although some critics argued that Büchner's superficiality and unfair weighing of evidence were marks of a dogmatic mind,[15] the real issue for most critics was what they called Büchner's "empirical dogmatism" or "dogmatic materialism."[16] These slogans—rhetorically akin to the "scientific dogmatism" discussed in Chapter 4—conveyed worry about a philosophy that rigorously reduced all morality and religion to their physical substrates, while at the same time displaying striking ignorance of Kant's critique of dogmatism (the latter point being emphasized by Friedrich Albert Lange in particular).[17] The Materialism Controversy, accordingly, did not focus on Büchner's personal virtues and vices but on a materialist worldview that was seen as no less dogmatic than the theological doctrine and Idealist philosophy ("the dogmatism of speculative concepts") that it sought to replace.[18]

If this makes the case of Büchner different from the examples of Ranke and Froude, it does resemble how Auguste Comte, the French positivist, and Cesare Lombroso, the Italian criminologist, acquired notoriety as dogmatic thinkers. The Victorian critics who compared Comte to Hobbes did so, partly because they interpreted both men as distancing themselves from all revealed

---

[12] Frederick C. Beiser, *After Hegel: German Philosophy, 1840–1900* (Oxford: Oxford University Press, 2014), 53–96.

[13] E. D. Fawcett, "Evidence and Impossibility: The Logic of a priori Negation and the Relations of the Subjective to the Objective in the Estimation of Evidence," *The Path* 2 (1887): 108–14, at 111.

[14] Karl Pearson, "The Prostitution of Science" (1887), in Pearson, *The Ethic of Freethought: A Selection of Essays and Lectures* (London: T. Fisher Unwin, 1888), 33–53, at 40; Theodore M. Porter, *Karl Pearson: The Scientific Life in a Statistical Age* (Princeton: Princeton University Press, 2004), 197, 199, 206.

[15] "Bain on the Senses and the Intellect," *The Anthropological Review* 2 (1864): 250–62, at 253.

[16] For example, Adolph Cornill, *Materialismus und Idealismus in ihren gegenwärtigen Entwickelungskrisen* (Heidelberg: J. C. B. Mohr, 1858), 147; Friedrich Albert Lange, *Geschichte des Materialismus und Kritik seiner Bedeutung in der Gegenwart* (Iserlohn: J. Baedeker, 1866), 272.

[17] Lange, *Geschichte des Materialismus*, esp. 270–3.

[18] Cornill, *Materialismus und Idealismus*, 144.

religion, but partly also because Comte presented his positivist philosophy with the same lack of humility that had struck Victorian readers in Hobbes ("The modesty of Locke is as evident as the haughtiness and dogmatism of Hobbes").[19] Indeed, "absolute rigidity" was what Annie Besant, a British women's rights activist and author of a book on Comte, found most remarkable about Comte's thinking—a trait that she, too, was quick to interpret in papal terms ("Comte's mind was essentially Roman Catholic, although he believed in no God; he is an infallible Pope under a new name, with a new creed on his lips, with dogma in one hand, and excommunication in the other").[20] Likewise, the German philosopher Georg Mehlis argued that Comtean positivism was "dogmatic" in that it declared: "This must be and cannot be different." Dogmatic, too, was Comte's quasi-religious appreciation of science and his (surprisingly non-scientific) refusal to subject his bold hypotheses to critical scrutiny. In Comte's hands, concluded Mehlis, all *Wissenschaft* becomes *Dogma.*[21]

Similar charges were brought against Lombroso's branch of positivism. Although an Italian admirer hailed the criminologist as an innovator who "had brought a fresh breath of renewal and modernity" into a world "stifled by dogma,"[22] critics like the psychiatrist Clodomiro Bonfigli accused Lombroso of elevating a disputable theory about the inherited nature of criminality into a seemingly unquestionable dogma (thereby unveiling his aspiration to "papacy in science"—the papal analogy was everywhere).[23] On similar grounds, the German critics Robert Sommer and Reinhard Frank disapproved of the "dogmatic conceptions" and "essential dogma of the Lombroso school": they simply did not believe that criminal conduct could as straightforwardly be reduced to genetic factors as Lombroso maintained.[24]

Finally, to return to the German historians who introduced the trope of "Rankean objectivity," Otto von Bismarck's anti-Catholic *Kulturkampf* prompted

---

[19] Bowen, *Modern Philosophy*, 4.

[20] Annie Besant, *Auguste Comte: His Philosophy, His Religion, and His Sociology* (London: C. Watts, 1889), 29–30.

[21] Georg Mehlis, *Die Geschichtsphilosophie Auguste Comtes kritisch dargestellt* (Leipzig: F. Eckardt, 1909), 18, 158, 118.

[22] Mario Pilo, "Filosofia scientifica e filosofia verbale," *Il pensiero nuovo* 1 (1898): 11–23, at 13.

[23] Clordomiro Bonfigli, *Sulla pellagra: lettere polemiche dirette al chiarissimo Sig. Dottor C. Lombroso* . . . ([Forlì]: [Tipografia Democratica], [1878]), 12, 6. David G. Horn, *The Criminal Body: Lombroso and the Anatomy of Deviance* (New York: Routledge, 2003), 171 n. 48 mentions some other religious titles attributed to Lombroso ("false prophet," "founder of a new religion").

[24] Robert Sommer, *Kriminalpsychologie und strafrechtliche Psychopathologie auf naturwissenschaftlicher Grundlage* (Leipzig: J. A. Barth, 1904), 320; Reinhard Frank, *Vergeltungsstrafe und Schutzstrafe: Die Lehre Lombrosos: Zwei Vorträge* (Tübingen: J. C. B. Mohr, 1908), 33. What complicated matters, and puzzled not a few commentators, was that Comte himself often used the term "dogmatism" in a positive sense. We will return to this in Chapter 6.

the Protestant majority among them to frame dogmatism as a vice to which especially Catholic historians were prone. Indeed, in their eyes, no one more tangibly embodied dogmatism than Johannes Janssen, the Catholic author of an eight-volume history of Germany that infuriated Protestant readers with its thesis that the Lutheran Reformation had been more of a curse than a blessing for the German people. In response, a contingent of Protestant historians led by Friedrich Nippold began to ridicule, scorn, and belittle "objectivity à la Janssen."[25] They accused the Catholic historian of dogmatism—especially of loyalty to an infallible pope, which they saw as incompatible with unbiased historical scholarship—as well as tendentiousness (a "tendentious assembling of quotations," as one scholar put it).[26] When Janssen answered his critics in print, the assaults only intensified, as a result of which "the Janssen method" became a phrase with almost proverbial status.[27] It even found its way into unrelated contexts, such as the controversy over the Seven Years' War prompted by the work of Albert Naudé. "Like Janssen," judged Max Lehmann in 1894, Naudé "approaches his subject matter with a preconceived opinion; he only sees evidence for dogmas that he treats as certain from the beginning; he ignores everything that contradicts them."[28] Janssen (followed by Naudé) thus resembled Froude in personifying a habit of mind that scholars rejected as a vice. Also, his case illustrates once again that when charges of dogmatism were being made, science and religion debates of the sort discussed in Chapter 4 were seldom far away.

*   *   *

Anti-Catholic images were, of course, not the only stereotypes common among nineteenth-century scholars. Apart from clichéd images of the Near

---

[25] Friedrich Nippold, "Literarisch-kritischer Anhang," in Nippold (ed.), *Berner Beiträge zur Geschichte der Schweizerischen Reformationskirchen* (Bern: K. J. Wyß, 1884), 414–54, at 417; "Romanismus und deutsch-christlicher Katholicismus," *Protestantische Kirchenzeitung für das evangelische Deutschland* 33 (1887): 267–79, at 275; "Die Zukunftsaufgabe der interconfessionellen Forschung als vergleichender Confessionsgeschichte: Sendschreiben an Dr. von Döllinger" (1888), in Nippold, *Katholisch oder jesuitisch? Drei zeitgeschichtliche Untersuchungen* (Leipzig: Georg Reichardt, 1888), 161–213, at 172.

[26] Friedrich Nippold, *Handbuch der neuesten Kirchengeschichte*, 3rd ed., vol. 2 (Elberfeld: R. L. Friderichs, 1883), 795; Hans Delbrück, "Historische Methode," *Preußische Jahrbücher* 53 (1884): 529–50, at 544.

[27] Nippold, *Handbuch*, 793.

[28] Max Lehmann, *Friedrich der Grosse und der Ursprung des Siebenjährigen Krieges* (Leipzig: S. Hirzel, 1894), 139. Similarly, Hans Delbrück, "Ueber den Ursprung des Siebenjährigen Krieges (Nachtrag)," *Preußische Jahrbücher* 86 (1896): 416–27, at 417–18 and, in the context of the so-called *Lamprechtstreit*, G. v[on] Below, "Die neue historische Methode," *Historische Zeitschrift* 81 (1898): 193–273, at 228, 240.

and Far East that testified to the existence of what Edward Said called an "Orientalist gaze,"[29] national stereotypes exerted tremendous influence, also on how scholars perceived the work of their colleagues abroad. If even historical handbooks presented "measurement, calculation, and classification" as typically French qualities, "completeness and thoroughness of research" as German virtues, and "strong individualism" as a distinctively English trait,[30] it comes as no surprise that book reviewers and obituary writers also interpreted individual character traits as mirrors of national character traits. Emil du Bois-Reymond, for instance, was described as a mixture of "Celtic fervour with Teutonic thoroughness," while Thomas Edison was called "French in his brilliance, more than German in his thoroughness, [and] . . . totally American in the application of his genius to practical ends."[31] This prompts the question: To what extent was dogmatism, too, perceived as typical for one country more than another?

Although Italian authors sometimes complained about "French dogmatism," while others believed the Scots were suffering from the "national vice of dogmatism,"[32] Germany was the country most frequently associated with dogmatism. Originating in the early nineteenth century, the trope of "German dogmatism" gained momentum especially after the Franco-Prussian War and during the First World War.[33] Félix Gaffiot's 1916 polemics against his German colleagues are a case in point. Gaffiot was a French Latinist who believed that Latin grammar and syntax had been much less rigid than what modern students learned at school. Unlike some of his French colleagues, who dared to correct even Cicero or Livy for violating syntactical rules, Gaffiot maintained that the classics knew a "true Latin," of which modern textbook rules were only poor approximations.[34] If this critique had initially been targeted at French classicists, the Great War provided Gaffiot with an occasion for highlighting Germany's contribution to grammatical system building. Due to their national fondness for "tight rules," German classicists had codified the Latin language

---

[29] Edward W. Said, *Orientalism* (Harmondsworth: Penguin, 1978).

[30] John Theodore Merz, *A History of European Thought in the Nineteenth Century*, vol. 1 (Edinburgh: Blackwood, 1896), 298, 213, 286.

[31] John G. McKendrick, "Human Electricity," *The Fortnightly Review* 51 (1892): 634–41, at 636; N. N., "Thomas Alva Edison," *The Engineering Magazine* 50 (1915): 199. These examples are discussed at greater length in Herman Paul, "German Thoroughness in Baltimore: Epistemic Virtues and National Stereotypes," *History of Humanities* 3, no. 2 (2018): 327–50.

[32] Giovanni Gavazzi-Spech, *Sulla libertà di stampa; pensieri* (Milan: Fratelli Dumolard, 1881), 328; N. N., "La Conferenza di Berna per la protezione della proprièta letteraria ed artistica," *Bibliografia italiana* 20 (1886): 57–8, at 58; N. N., "Notes," *The Nation* 10 (1870): 175–7, at 176.

[33] An example from shortly after the Franco-Prussian War is [François] Moigno, *Religion et patrie vengées de la fausse science et de l'envie haineuse* (Paris: Les Mondes, 1872), 4.

[34] Félix Gaffiot, *Pour le vrai Latin*, vol. 1 (Paris: Ernest Leroux, 1909).

without any apprehension for its "suppleness" (which, of course, French *ésprit de finesse* knew much better how to appreciate).[35] Interestingly, Gaffiot not only called for liberation from this German dogmatism—"Let's shake off the yoke"—but also offered a quasi-psychological explanation of it. The Germans, said Gaffiot, prefer obedience to rules over the exercise of their own minds; they need directions and sometimes even authoritative guidance. However, such "regulation" and "organization" leave little room for independent scholarly thinking. As a result, "dogmatism is, with rare exceptions, the common trait of German philologists and grammarians."[36]

Gaffiot's analysis was hardly original: similar commonplaces can be found in other wartime musings on the ills of German *Wissenschaft*.[37] The French chemist Armand Gautier, for instance, expressed a broadly held opinion in describing the German mind as "methodical," "essentially deductive," and "ruthlessly logical." It was eminently able to think through all the implications of a scientific idea but rarely produced fruitful new ideas itself.[38] According to the zoologist Louis-Félix Henneguy, academic hierarchies in Germany contributed to this one-sidedness: German professors expected their students to accept their own doctrines as if they were "intangible dogmas," immune to critique.[39] Drawing on an older polemical booklet with the telling title *Der Professor ist die deutsche Nationalkrankheit* (The Professor is the German National Disease), an article in *La Grande Revue* agreed that the German educational system "killed all personal initiative in intelligent students," thereby producing "a people docile and robust, firmly attached to national institutions."[40] Elsewhere in Europe, these twin vices of docility and dogmatism were also recognized as characteristic defects, not merely of German scholars, but of the German population at large. The Irish-born educationalist Edmond Holmes even devoted an entire book to "ultra-dogmatism" and "ultra-docility" as German

---

[35] Félix Gaffiot, "Le dogmatisme allemand et les études latines," *Revue universitaire* 25 (1916): 334–6, at 336.

[36] Ibid., 336, 335.

[37] Andreas Kleinert, "Von der science allemande zur deutschen Physik: Nationalismus und moderne Naturwissenschaft in Frankreich und Deutschland zwischen 1914 and 1940," *Francia* 6 (1978): 509–25.

[38] Armand Gautier, "La science et l'esprit allemands," in Gabriel Petit and Maurice Leudet (eds.), *Les Allemands et la science* (Paris Félix Alcan, 1916), 167–77, at 168.

[39] F. Henneguy, "L'Allemagne et les sciences biologiques," ibid., 205–17, at 215.

[40] H. Fritel-Cordelet, "Der Professor ist die deutsche Nationalkrankheit," *La Grande Revue* 88 (1915): 545–52, at 547, 551. The English translation is taken from Martha Hanna, *The Mobilization of Intellect: French Scholars and Writers during the Great War* (Cambridge, MA: Harvard University Press, 1996), 96.

character traits ("The docility of the German people is equalled only by their dogmatism").[41]

If these examples show that Galliot was not alone in perceiving dogmatism as a typical German vice, it would, nonetheless, be unwarranted to conclude that "German dogmatism" occupied a privileged position in French views of German *Wissenschaft*. As Martha Hanna and others have shown, dogmatism was one of a range of vices that French scholars during the Great War attributed to their colleagues across the Rhine. Just as common were charges of mechanism, determinism, materialism, authoritarianism, and obscurity (alongside admiration for German accuracy and meticulousness).[42] The "metaphysical instinct" of German science, paired with its dislike of French *bon sens* and habit of mistaking obscurity for profoundness of insight, was also a common theme.[43] Moreover, it is worth observing that some of the most influential anti-German treatises—Pierre Duhem's *German Science* (1915), for instance—did not devote a single word to "German dogmatism."[44] Therefore, even if a number of French war-induced propaganda texts depicted German academics as prone to dogmatic thinking, the link between the country and the vice was not mutually exclusive.

*   *   *

An even grimmer stereotype was that of "Jewish dogmatism" as popularized by Johannes Stark. Three years after receiving the Nobel Prize in Physics, Stark published a pamphlet on *The Current Crisis in German Physics* (1922), in which he accused two of the most fertile minds in theoretical physics, Albert Einstein and Arnold Sommerfeld, of bringing German physics into disrepute. The problem was initially presented as a methodological one: neither quantum theory nor Einstein's relativity theory could lay claim to experimental verification. Stark's polemical tone, however, was also a response to Einstein's supposedly un-German internationalism and unpatriotic lecturing in Paris, only years after the Treaty of Versailles. Stark, in other words, was not only a hard-

[41] Edmond Holmes, *The Nemesis of Docility: A Study of German Character* (London: Constable & Company, 1916), 48, 78.

[42] Hanna, *Mobilization of Intellect*, 92, 186; Harry W. Paul, *The Sorcerer's Apprentice: The French Scientist's Image of German Science, 1840–1919* (Gainesville: University of Florida Press, 1972), 40–3.

[43] For example, Réne Lote, "Rôle national de la science allemande: l'université dans l'état," in Petit and Leudet, *Les Allemands et la science*, 251–62, at 259, drawing on Lote, *Les origines mystiques de la science "allemande"* (Paris: Félix Alcan, 1913).

[44] Pierre Duhem, *La science allemande* (Paris: A. Hermann & Fils, 1915).

nosed empiricist but also a chauvinist who expected German physicists to identify with the national cause.[45]

After joining the Nazi Party (NSDAP) in 1930, Stark added a dose of anti-Semitism to his attacks on theoretical physics. He did so by contrasting true "Germanic research, which is oriented toward reality," with a "Jewish mentality" that he saw typified by "intellectualism, dogmatic formalism, and propagandistic commercialism."[46] While propagandism was a sneer at Einstein's fame and, more specifically, his frequent appearance on the speakers' circuit, the first two ills referred to the abstractions of quantum theory and general relativity. Had theoretical physics already been framed as un-German, it now appeared more specifically as Jewish (an implicit reference to Einstein and others' Jewish family backgrounds). An English-language article published in Nature in 1938 put it even more bluntly. There are, said Stark, "two principal types of mentality in physics": a pragmatic Aryan mentality, committed to patiently unraveling the secrets of nature, and a "dogmatic spirit," characterized by idle theorizing, that manifests itself predominantly among the "Jews in German science." If we remember, added Stark, "that Jews played a decisive part in the foundation of theological dogmatism, and that the authors and propagandists of Marxian and communist dogmas are for the most part Jews, we must establish and recognize the fact that the natural inclination to dogmatic thought appears with especial frequency in people of Jewish origin."[47]

Internationally, this outburst of anti-Semitism did not remain unchallenged. In the pages of Nature, Arthur Eve retorted that "the whole theory of pragmatists and dogmatists is pure moonshine."[48] Even in Nazi Germany, protests were voiced, though not always in public. Despite some physicists agreeing that German "science has burdened itself with an apparently increasingly home-grown dogmatism,"[49] others denounced Stark's contrast between Aryan pragmatism and Jewish dogmatism as "completely arbitrary"

---

[45] Johannes Stark, Die gegenwärtige Krisis in der deutschen Physik (Leipzig: Johann Ambrosius Barth, 1922), 8–9, 15.

[46] Johannes Stark, "Die 'Wissenschaft' versagte politisch," Das Schwarze Korps 28 (1937): 6, quoted from the English translation in Klaus Hentschel (ed.), Physics and National Socialism: An Anthology of Primary Sources, trans. Ann M. Hentschel (Basel: Birkhäuser Verlag, 1996), 157–60, at 158.

[47] J. Stark, "The Pragmatic and the Dogmatic Spirit in Physics," Nature 141, no. 3574 (1938): 770–2, at 770, 771, 772. Stark elaborated on the theme in a Munich lecture published in Johannes Stark and Wilhelm Müller, Jüdische und deutsche Physik: Vorträge zur Eröffnung des Kolloquiums für theoretische Physik an der Universität München (Leipzig: Heling, 1941).

[48] A. S. Eve, "Foundations of Physics," Nature 142, no. 3602 (1938): 857–9, at 858.

[49] Wilhelm Müller, "Die Lage der theoretischen Physik an den Universitäten," Zeitschrift für die gesamte Naturwissenschaft 6, nos. 11–12 (1940): 281–98, quoted from the English translation in Hentschel, Physics and National Socialism, 246–59, at 247.

and "unproven."[50] As theoretical physicist Walter Weizel put it in 1942: "It is completely unscientific to suspect quantum theory of being Jewish."[51] Nonetheless, the fact that Weizel felt compelled to add that this view was shared by the entire Faculty of Science and Mathematics at the University of Bonn, where he taught, speaks volumes about the risks of challenging the trope of Jewish dogmatism in a country under Nazi rule.[52]

* * *

If the two previous chapters showed that dogmatism had strong connotations of pastness and clerical authority, the stereotypical attributions examined in this chapter were significantly less robust. Although some individuals acquired a reputation for dogmatism, sometimes even to the point of lending their name to it, their number was small. Moreover, insofar as they served as anti-models or as warning examples of how virtues could turn into vices, they did so only during their lifetimes, in one discipline, and not beyond the borders of their own country or language. National stereotypes were more broadly used: "German dogmatism" circulated as widely as "Soviet dogmatism" would do in the Cold War era (Chapter 8). Like Stark's "Jewish dogmatism," these national stereotypes found their widest application in times of conflict, under circumstances that prompted scholars to renegotiate the boundaries between in- and out-groups.

Two larger insights can be derived from this. The first is that charges of dogmatism as examined in the last three chapters often served causes larger than a scientific line of research. When scholars found themselves accused of dogmatism, this typically happened in relation to big issues like scientific progress, science and religion, national identity, and racial purity. Also, while *Dogmatismus* appeared as a word of abuse in the most varied of scholarly debates, it gained special traction in controversies that far exceeded normal academic disagreement: in the Darwinian controversies, during Bismarck *Kulturkampf*, in the context of the First World War, and in

---

[50] Carl Ramsauer, "Die Widerlegung der Vorwürfe gegen die moderne theoretische Physik als ein angebliches Erzeugnis jüdischen Geistes" (unpublished, submitted to the Reich Education Ministry in 1940), quoted from the English translation in Hentschel, *Physics and National Socialism*, 285–9, at 286.

[51] Walter Weizel, review of *Jüdische und deutsche Physik* by Johannes Stark and Wilhelm Müller, *Zeitschrift für technische Physik* 23, no. 1 (1942): 25, quoted from the English translation in Hentschel, *Physics and National Socialism*, 276–7, at 277.

[52] For more background and context, see Ian D. Beyerchen, *Scientists under Hitler: Politics and the Physics Community in the Third Reich* (New Haven: Yale University Press, 1977), 103–22, and Dieter Hoffmann and Mark Walker (eds.), *Physiker zwischen Autonomie und Anpassung: Die Deutsche Physikalische Gesellschaft im Dritten Reich* (Weinheim: Wiley-VCH, 2007).

the anti-Semitic rhetoric of German National-Socialists. Like other value-laden rhetorical figures—think of the Mammon metaphor ("Ye cannot serve God and mammon") as utilized in academic quarrels against a perceived commercialization of science—dogmatism was invoked especially in contexts where scholars found themselves writing not only as researchers but also as citizens, patriots, believers, or guardians of academic integrity.[53]

If this observation is correct, it may help explain why dogmatism's connotations of pastness and religious authority were stronger than the stereotypes examined in this chapter. The "Janssen method" made little sense to non-historians, just as the rigidity of German Latinists and the non-experimental physics of Einstein and Sommerfeld were too specific to serve as broadly recognizable examples of dogmatism. By contrast, clinging to superannuated theories was a phenomenon observable across disciplinary and geographical borders, just as scholars in every field of study encountered science and religion debates. While the princes of dogmatists featured in this chapter could serve as embodiments of vice in specific scholarly communities, their rhetorical power did not equal the strength of narratives of progress that told nineteenth-century men of science to keep discovering new truths, unrestrained by convention or clerical authority.

---

[53] For example, John Tyndall, *Lectures on Light: Delivered in the United States in 1872–'73* (New York: D. Appleton and Company, 1873), 189; James Lewis Howe, "The Aim and Future of Natural Science," *Science* 16, no. 404 (1890): 239–44; James Taft Hatfield, "Scholarship and the Commonwealth," *PMLA* 17, no. 3 (1902): 391–409, at 394; William Osler, *Aequanimitas: With Other Addresses to Medical Students, Nurses and Practitioners of Medicine* (London: L. K. Hewis, 1904), 29.

6

Dogmatism

Non-Pejorative Meanings

Judging by the previous chapters, scholars in nineteenth- and early twentieth-century Europe almost without exception perceived of dogmatism as a scholarly vice. Regardless of whether they saw it embodied in specific individuals (Chapter 5) or warned more generally against its dangers, they equated dogmatism with a character trait that was harmful to the pursuit of learning. In most cases, critics depicting this evil as a relic of the past (Chapter 3) agreed with authors emphasizing the term's religious connotations (Chapter 4) that "dogmatism" was antithetical to the virtues required for scholarly research. Dogmatism, in other words, was framed as a threat to scientific integrity because it was a vice instead of a virtue. As such, the term usually had an accusatory ring to it. For most of the authors cited so far, "dogmatism" was a pejorative phrase that they attributed for polemical purposes to intellectual opponents. It was never a neutral term, let alone a badge of honor or an object of aspiration.

This notion of dogmatism as a scholarly vice, however, never managed to drive all competitors out of circulation. Several older meanings of the term (surveyed in Chapter 2) persisted in its shadow. This is especially true for the idea of dogmatic thinking serving as a necessary supplement to historical thinking and for the notion of dogmatic teaching. What distinguished these older notions from the vice that most nineteenth-century authors understood dogmatism to be was their positive valuation of dogmatic thinking. Dogmatism allowed for inductive reasoning, thereby enabling scholars to discern patterns in their material. Also, it had didactic value insofar as it offered a systematic overview of existing knowledge. Although these older meanings had been driven into marginality by the rise to prominence of dogmatism as a vice, they occasionally found their way back into the discussion. This chapter will look at some of these moments, starting with three interventions by high-profile thinkers and continuing with a decades-long debate on science education in which several less prominent figures made their voices heard. To what extent, we ask, did their retrievals of older meanings challenge the hegemony of dogmatism as a vice?

* * *

Auguste Comte is perhaps the best-known example of a thinker for whom dogmatism was not a vice but an aspiration. Like many others at the time, the French philosopher and sociologist structured his methodological thoughts around the old distinction between historical and dogmatic modes of analysis (Chapter 2). When nineteenth-century historians, philologists, or biblical scholars invoked this pair of terms, they usually did so in support of a historical method of which source criticism and contextual sensitivity were the principal marks. The dogmatic method, by contrast, was dismissed as ahistorical, uncritical, and prejudiced.[1] Comte, however, construed the contrast differently. Sticking closer to the terms' original meanings, he identified the dogmatic method with a systematic, synthesizing mode of thinking that brings order to a wealth of material that the historical method can only present chronologically, "in the same order in which it was actually obtained by the human mind." Typical of the dogmatic method, then, is that "the system of ideas is presented as it might be conceived of at this day, by a mind which, duly prepared and placed at the right point of view, should begin to reconstitute the science as a whole." Dogmatic reasoning so defined is not a vice but an intellectual operation that contributes mightily to the progress of scientific understanding.[2]

Second, although Comte saw the historical method as inferior to the dogmatic one, he emphasized that the latter can be applied only once the former has done its work. There is, in other words, a temporal sequence, both in a scholar's individual work and in the project of science at large. As for the first point, Comte's correspondence contains a letter to a friend in which he urges patience. No one has ever grasped a problem dogmatically at

---

[1] Paul Michael Kurtz, "A Historical, Critical Retrospective on Historical Criticism," in Ian Boxall and Bradley C. Gregory (eds.), *The New Cambridge Companion to Biblical Interpretation* (Cambridge: Cambridge University Press, 2022), 15–36; Herman Paul, "Virtue Language in Nineteenth-Century Orientalism: A Case Study in Historical Epistemology," *Modern Intellectual History* 13, no. 3 (2017): 689–715.

[2] Auguste Comte, *The Positive Philosophy of Auguste Comte*, trans. Harriet Martineau, vol. 1 (London: John Chapman, 1853), 23. Although Martineau's translation is notoriously inaccurate, here it follows the French original quite closely: Auguste Comte, *Cours de philosophie positive*, vol. 1 (Paris: Rouen frères, 1830), 77.

once; everyone always starts historically, with bits and pieces of insight that only after lots of time allow themselves to be ordered systematically.[3] On the other hand, Comte left no doubt that the eventual ambition of science is to reach such a dogmatic stage. "As we advance to a higher position in science," he wrote, the dogmatic method gradually supersedes the historical one.[4] In an early text, from the mid-1820s, Comte even went so far as to claim that "*dogmatism* is the normal state of the human mind, the state to which by nature it tends, continuously and in all sorts."[5] Dogmatic understanding, for Comte, thus amounted to an aspiration that cannot be immediately realized, yet defines the epistemic task at hand.

Comte is, of course, best known for his so-called law of three stages, according to which human knowledge proceeds from a theological phase via a metaphysical stage to a state of positive knowledge, in which the world is explained scientifically instead of mythologically or metaphysically. Anticipating this third and final stage, Comte himself tried to analyze the world as dogmatically as possible—that is, systematically rather than historically. Whatever the branch of science, political ideology, or religious worldview that he discussed, Comte's modus operandi was to identify its leading dogmas. Consequently, his writings abound with phrases like "the dogma of invariability," "the dogma of humanity," "the dogma of equality," "the dogma of liberty of conscience," and "the famous theologico-metaphysical dogma of optimism."[6]

To many readers, such non-pejorative talk of dogmas and dogmatism was a cause of confusion. In his explanatory notes to the British translation of *A Discourse on the Positive Spirit* (1844), Edward Spencer Beesley, a former president of the London Positivist Society, alerted his readers to the peculiarity of Comte's terminology: "The word Dogma, when used by Comte of any positive doctrine, of course does not imply that it rests—like, for instance, the Catholic doctrine of Transubstantiation—on authority as opposed to experience or demonstration, but only that it is being treated, for educational purposes, as firmly established."[7] What added to the confusion was that Comte's commitment to "dogmatic thinking," in his own definition

---

[3] Auguste Comte to Gustave d'Eichthal, June 6, 1824, in Comte, *Correspondance générale et confessions*, vol. 1, ed. Paulo E. de Berrêdo Carneiro and Pierre Arnaud (Paris: Mouton, 1973), 93–8, at 95.

[4] Comte, *Positive Philosophy*, vol. 1, 23.

[5] Auguste Comte, "Considerations of the Spiritual Power" (1825–6), in Comte, *Early Political Writings*, trans. H. S. Jones (Cambridge: Cambridge University Press, 1998), 187–227, at 214.

[6] Auguste Comte, *System of Positive Philosophy*, vol. 4, trans. Richard Congreve and Henry Dix Hutton (London: Longmans, Green, and Co., 1877), 158, 171–2, 422, 533, 575.

[7] Auguste Comte, *A Discourse on the Positive Spirit*, trans. Edward Spencer Beesly (London: William Reeves, 1903), xii. See also Georg Mehlis, *Die Geschichtsphilosophie Auguste Comtes kritisch dargestellt* (Leipzig: F. Eckardt, 1909), 3.

of the term, was widely perceived as reflecting a dogmatic habit of mind in a more conventional sense of the word. Sometimes it was his law of three stages that was called dogmatic ("a gratuitous *a priori* dogmatism").[8] On other occasions, it was Comte himself who was called "over-dogmatic."[9] As we saw in Chapter 5, the French positivist was one of those "princes of dogmatism" whom nineteenth-century readers saw embodying the vice of dogmatism more clearly than anyone else. His dogmatic inclinations were judged to be no weaker than Hobbes' or the pope's. "No writer, either of early or of recent date," wrote John Stuart Mill, "is chargeable in a higher degree with this aberration from the true scientific spirit, than M. Comte."[10]

Comte's attempt to breathe new life into an old pair of words did, consequently, not meet with much enthusiasm. Although some French disciples faithfully adopted the master's terminology,[11] the overall appeal of Comte's revaluation of dogmatic thinking was limited. Most commentators were more concerned about the dogmatic pose that Comte adopted than impressed by his attempt to salvage the term from its pejorative connotations.

*   *   *

Comte was not the only philosopher who tried to counter the negative reputation of dogmatic reasoning. Each in his own way, the Spanish-American philosopher George Santayana, in the early decades of the twentieth century, and the American philosopher of science Thomas S. Kuhn, in the 1960s, also developed non-pejorative notions of dogmatism. Both, however, also provoked misunderstanding and opposition.

Santayana was one of the more colorful figures in early twentieth-century philosophy. Born in Spain and educated in the United States, Germany, and England, he was a Harvard professor in philosophy (1889–1912) before returning to Europe and settling in Rome. As early as 1905, Santayana showed himself to be unconvinced by the Whewellian view that dogmatism had become an outdated mode of thinking. "People speak of dogmatism as if it were a method to be altogether outgrown." This, however, ignores that human thinking

---

[8] R. R. Marett, review of *The Philosophy of Auguste Comte*, by Lucien Lévy-Bruhl, *The Economic Review* 14 (1904): 105–7, at 105.

[9] Godfrey Lushington as quoted in E. S. Beesly, "Sir Godfrey Lushington," *The Positivist Review* 15 (1907): 70–1, at 70.

[10] John Stuart Mill, *A System of Logic, Ratiocinative and Inductive . . .*, 3rd ed., vol. 2 (London: John W. Parker, 1851), 430. For Mill's assessment of Comte's philosophy, see also his *Auguste Comte and Positivism* (London: N. Trübner & Co., 1865).

[11] For example, É. Littré, *La science au point de vue philosophique* (Paris: Didier et cie., 1873), 10–11 and *Fragments de philosophie positive et de sociologie contemporaine* (Paris: La philosophie positive, 1876), 192, 248, 574, 598.

always rests on certain background beliefs. While one may challenge some of the dogmas of the day, one's alternative will still involve "assumptions and dogmas." If one would try to get rid of all of them, one would reach a point of silence: nothing can be thought or said without some tacit beliefs operating in the background.[12] Dogmas are, therefore, indispensable to the human mind. As Santayana himself declared on a later occasion: "Dogma cannot be abandoned; it can only be revised in view of some more elementary dogma which it has not yet occurred to the sceptic to doubt."[13] Santayana's dogmas, then, resembled Galen's δογματα as discussed in Chapter 2: they were postulates without which human beings cannot make sense of their experience.

Santayana wrote this at a time when the pragmatist philosopher John Dewey established himself as a major theorist of educational reform. One of the key features of Dewey's educational thinking was that it sought to ban all dogmatism for the sake of critical, scientific, or reflective thinking.[14] How hard Santayana's understanding of dogmatism was to reconcile with Dewey's is apparent from a series of published exchanges between the two men.[15] In a review of Dewey's *Experience and Nature* (1925), Santayana acknowledged the author's unrelenting struggle against dogmatism. "The typical philosopher's fallacy, in his eyes, has been the habit of hypostatizing the conclusions to which reflection may lead, and depicting them to be prior realities—the fallacy of dogmatism." This, however, did not prevent Santayana from speaking frankly, and non-pejoratively, about Dewey's own dogmas, such as his commitment to naturalistic metaphysics. To drive home the point that dogmas are unavoidable, he described himself as a "dogmatic naturalist."[16] As fellow American philosophers at the time did not fail to notice, this implied a rejection of Dewey's "pretension of avoiding dogmatism."[17] In response, Dewey claimed to agree with Santayana that everyone "must be dogmatic at some point in order to get anywhere with other matters."[18] He expressed

---

[12] George Santayana, *The Life of Reason or the Phases of Human Progress* (New York: Charles Scribner's Sons, 1905), 88.

[13] George Santayana, *Scepticism and Animal Faith: Introduction to a System of Philosophy* (New York: Charles Scribner's Sons, 1923), 8–9.

[14] Douglas J. Simpson, "John Dewey's Concept of the Dogmatic Thinker: Implications for the Teacher," *Journal of Philosophy and History of Education* 49 (1999): 159–72.

[15] A detailed analysis of this exchange is offered in Richard Marc Rubin, "Metaphysics as Morals: The Controversy between John Dewey and George Santayana" (PhD thesis, Washington University, 2000).

[16] George Santayana, "Dewey's Naturalistic Metaphysics," *The Journal of Philosophy* 22, no. 25 (1925): 673–88, at 675, 687.

[17] [Benjamin Ginzburg], "Philosophy," in Herbert Treadwell Wade (ed.), *The New International Year Book: A Compendium of the World's Progress for the Year 1925* (New York: Dodd, Mead, and Company, 1926), 554–7, at 556.

[18] John Dewey, "Half-Hearted Naturalism," *The Journal of Philosophy* 24, no. 3 (1927): 57–64, at 57.

his surprise, however, about Santayana using "'dogmatic' as a term of honor" rather than contempt.[19] Also, he argued that "even a dogmatist may be asked the grounds for his assertation, not, indeed, in the sense of what proof he has to offer, but in the sense of what is presupposed in the assertion, from what platform of beliefs it is proposed."[20] This is to say that Dewey, while rejecting the illusion of dogma-free thinking, still insisted on reducing dogmatic assumptions as much as possible—thereby holding to his own understanding of dogmatism as the vicious opposite of reflective thinking.[21]

If this case study shows us two philosophers talking at cross-purposes, something similar, or worse, happened after the publication of Thomas Kuhn's essay, "The Function of Dogma in Scientific Research" (1963). Originally delivered at an Oxford symposium in July 1961, when *The Structure of Scientific Revolutions* (1962) had not yet been published, the text offered a brief introduction to what Kuhn understood scientific paradigms to be, with special attention to the quasi-dogmatic ways in which students are socialized into them.[22] The premise of Kuhn's argument was that "nature is vastly too complex to be explored even approximately at random. Something must tell the scientist where to look and what to look for, and that something . . . is the paradigm with which his education as a scientist has supplied him." Partly, such paradigms are made up of background beliefs of the sort that Santayana called dogmas: beliefs about the sort of entities (atoms, molecules) that populate the world and the way these entities behave. Partly, also, paradigms consist of questions that scientists deem worth asking and the problems they single out for research.[23] While much of this remains implicit in everyday research, paradigms are made more explicit in teaching. "Scientific education," according to Kuhn, "inculcates what the scientific community had previously with difficulty gained—a deep commitment to a particular way of viewing the world and of practicing science in it." Accordingly, it is in teaching—in science textbooks, most notably—that "the dogmatism of mature science" becomes most visible. Insofar as students are being told what problems they should

---

[19] John Dewey, "Philosophy as a Fine Art," *The New Republic* 53 (1928): 352–4, reprinted in Dewey, *The Later Works, 1925–1953*, vol. 3, ed. Jo Ann Boydston (Carbondale: Southern Illinois University Press, 1984), 287–93, at 290.

[20] Dewey, "Half-Hearted Naturalism," 57.

[21] On Santayana's view that dogmatism can come in degrees, see *Life of Reason*, 88 and *Scepticism and Animal Faith*, 6–10.

[22] On the development of Kuhn's thought in these years, see James A. Marcum, *Thomas Kuhn's Revolution: An Historical Philosophy of Science* (London: Continuum, 2005), 43–51.

[23] Thomas S. Kuhn, "The Function of Dogma in Scientific Research," in A. C. Crombie (ed.), *Scientific Change: Historical Studies in the Intellectual, Social and Technical Conditions for Scientific Discovery and Technical Invention, from Antiquity to the Present* (London: Heinemann, 1963), 347–69, at 363, 359.

study, scientific education amounts to "a relatively dogmatic initiation into a pre-established problem-solving tradition that the student is neither invited nor equipped to evaluate."[24] On this account, dogmatism is not a scholarly vice but an effective method for familiarizing newcomers in the field with the scientific state of the art.

If we compare Kuhn's notion of dogmatism with Comte's and Santayana's, it is clear that Kuhn did anything but share Comte's appreciation of dogmatic thinking as a higher mode of understanding. He explicitly warned that neither dogmatism nor its counterpart—rebellion against inherited paradigms that, if successful, may result in paradigm change—should be understood as a "virtue."[25] Instead, for Kuhn, "scientific dogmatism" was a fact of life, without which modern science could not exist or be transmittable to new generations. If this quasi-sociological way of reasoning brought Kuhn close to Santayana, a key difference between the two was that Kuhn focused not on dogmas per se but on their transmission in education. Unlike Santayana, Kuhn drew attention to what early modern men of learning had called dogmatic teaching. Although it is unclear to what extent Kuhn was familiar with dogmatic medicine or dogmatic philosophy as defined in the seventeenth century, his argument was reminiscent of what early modern scholars had called a *methodus docendi et discendi* that sought to be systematic ("dogmatic") rather than historical. Finally, while Santayana, like most other authors featured in this book, attributed dogmatic beliefs to individuals, Kuhn was talking about dogmatism inherent to the science system as a whole. A commentator in the early 1970s put it well: "It is not that an individual scientist is dogmatic and inflexible, but, if Kuhn is right, it is normal science as such which is dogmatic."[26]

Given the negative connotations of dogmatism, which by the 1960s had only been strengthened by the rise of anti-authoritarian thinking (to be discussed in Chapter 7), it comes as no surprise that Kuhn's views met with opposition. Although philosophers of science spent more time debating Kuhn's ill-defined concept of paradigms than his understanding of dogmatism, several commentators wondered why Kuhn used the charged word "dogma."[27] In response, Kuhn conceded that this confusing term was better avoided.

---

[24] Ibid., 349, 351.

[25] Ibid., 349.

[26] R. Sundara Rajan, *Structure and Change in Philosophy* (Chennai: Centre of Advanced Study in Philosophy, 1974), 95–6.

[27] See, for example, Stephen Toulmin's and Edward Caldin's contributions to "Discussion," in Crombie, *Scientific Change*, 381–95, at 383, 385 and, in later decades, Leslie Sklair, *Organized Knowledge: A Sociological View of Science and Technology* (St. Albans: Hart-Davis MacGibbon, 1973), 131–2; William Hare, *In Defense of Open-mindedness* (Kingston: McGill-Queen's University Press, 1985), 83.

(Which indeed he did: he dropped it almost immediately from his vocabulary.)[28] Terminological issues aside, critics preferred normative questions over empirical ones. "Is the rigid narrow education described by Kuhn necessary to make good scientists?"[29] The geneticist Hiram Bentley Glass, answering this question in the negative, bluntly stated that he was "appalled to think that, if Mr. Kuhn is right, we should go back to teaching paradigms and dogmas, not as merely temporary expedients to aid us more clearly to visualize the nature of our scientific problems, but rather of the regular, approved method of scientific advance."[30] As Glass was deeply involved in curriculum studies and educational reform, his worry was that Kuhn's argument would legitimize the sort of dogmatic teaching that he and his colleagues did their best to fight.[31]

One of Kuhn's most formidable critics, Karl Popper, voiced a similar objection in arguing that "the 'normal' scientist, as described by Kuhn, has been badly taught. He has been taught in a dogmatic spirit: he is a victim of indoctrination." Accordingly, Popper did not think that Kuhn's normal science was normal at all. "I can only say that I see a very great danger in it . . .: a danger to science and, indeed, to our civilization."[32] As exaggerated as these last words may seem, they reflect the hope, widely shared in the 1960s, that the scientific ethos would have beneficial effects beyond the science classroom. For Glass, Popper, and others at the time, critical, anti-dogmatic thinking was a sine qua non for science and for the democratic cause as defined in the Cold War. Such a project left little room for non-pejorative notions of dogmatism, let alone for non-dismissive accounts of dogmatic science teaching.

*   *   *

By the time Kuhn, Glass, and Popper crossed swords about the promises and perils of dogmatic teaching, the topic already had a respectable history. Ever since the seventeenth century, men of learning had reflected on it, often on the premise that a systematic ordering of knowledge had unmistakable

---

[28] See Kuhn's response to critics in "Discussion," 392; Georg Reisch, "When *Structure* Met Sputnik: On the Cold War Origins of *The Structure of Scientific Revolutions*," in Naomi Oreskes and John Krige (eds.), *Science and Technology in the Global Cold War* (Cambridge, MA: MIT Press, 2014), 371–92, at 383–4.

[29] E. W. Hamburger, "Physics and Recent Trends in Education," in John L. Lewis (ed.), *New Trends in Physics Teaching*, vol. 3 (Paris: UNESCO, 1976), 212–23, at 219.

[30] "Discussion," 382.

[31] Reisch, "When *Structure* Met Sputnik," 379–82.

[32] Karl Popper, "Normal Science and Its Dangers," in Imre Lakatos and Alan Musgrave (eds.), *Criticism and the Growth of Knowledge: Proceedings of the International Colloquium in the Philosophy of Science, London, 1965*, vol. 4 (Cambridge: Cambridge University Press, 1970), 51–8, at 53.

didactic advantages. In the course of the nineteenth century, however, this had begun to change. When science in Whewell's sense of the word established itself as a powerful force, both in universities and in the world at large, "science education" became a theme to which both scientists and educators devoted much thought.[33] Many of their debates were not nearly as high-profile as the philosophical treatises cited earlier in this chapter. Science education was a theme discussed in school teachers' associations, cultural monthlies, and newspapers—though also, with perhaps surprising frequency, in a journal like *Nature*, because of its ambition to cover all science-related news.[34] A brief survey of dogmatic teaching as discussed under the umbrella of science education, from shortly after Comte's death until the rise to dominance of Dewey-inspired progressive education, shows a pattern similar to the philosophical one. Dogmatic teaching had its defenders, but their voices did not carry far in a climate that saw leading educational figures publish books with titles like *Deliver Us from Dogma* (a twentieth-century version, one might say, of Joseph Glanvill's *The Vanity of Dogmatizing*).[35]

As early as 1869, the British chemist Edmund James Mills observed that the advance of scientific knowledge, usually hailed as a blessing, could be a challenge for science teachers, especially in secondary schools. "The rapid progress of experimental discovery," he wrote, amounts to a serious "obstacle to the elementary teaching of any scientific subject."[36] Part of the problem lay with the teachers: How could they keep their syllabi up-to-date when new theories and hypotheses were put forward on an almost daily basis? A more serious problem, however, was children's ability to acquaint themselves with science without receiving any "dogmatic" instruction in the form of lectures about established facts or theories. Would it be possible for teachers to instill a "scientific habit" in their students by avoiding such dogmatic teaching, encouraging children, instead, to make their own observations and draw their own conclusions?

One possible answer came from the vice president of the Geological Society of America, Alexander Winchell. In an 1884 article, Winchell pointed out that teaching methods must be differentiated according to students' level of ability. "The *ratiocinative* process of acquisition should be promoted in all cases; but where the powers of the learner are incapable of seizing the

---

[33] W. H. Brock, "Science Education," in R. C. Olby et al. (eds.), *Companion to the History of Modern Science* (London: Routledge, 1990), 946–59.

[34] Melinda Baldwin, *Making Nature: The History of a Scientific Journal* (Chicago: University of Chicago Press, 2015), 30–7.

[35] Alvin Johnson, *Deliver Us from Dogma* (New York: American Association for Adult Education, 1934). We owe this reference to Edurne De Wilde.

[36] E. J. Mills, "Barff's Handbook of Chemistry," *Nature* 1, no. 80 (1869): 80.

generalization, it must be enunciated *dogmatically*." Thinking like a scientist—making observations, comparisons, inferences, and generalizations—was, in other words, a noble objective but not a realistic goal for children unfamiliar with the basics of science. More controversially, Winchell added that even advanced students will get stuck when their teachers try to avoid dogmatic teaching at all costs. "To denounce all dogmatic statement of general principles, is to assume that the tottering intellect of the young learner is capable of drawing the same generalizations as have been framed by the sturdiest efforts of experts, and this is a baseless assumption." Consequently, for Winchell, dogmatic teaching had a legitimate place in science education simply because it was didactically unavoidable.[37]

Winchell's views, however, did not remain uncontested. In science-minded journals like *Nature*, it became more common for authors to speak condescendingly about "soul-destroying" textbooks, to reject a "dogmatic exposition of the elementary laws of chemistry," or to warn more broadly against "any dogmatic exposition of ideas."[38] The rationale behind this aversion was made explicit by a critic of Daniel Trembly MacDougal's textbook on plant physiology: "The elementary, no less than the more advanced, student requires to be made at the outset to *think for himself*."[39] Notwithstanding such firm anti-dogmatic stances, even the pages of *Nature* saw different authors reaching different conclusions. Commenting on a textbook by George Neil Stewart, a former student of the Edinburgh professors Peter Guthrie Tait and William Rutherford, the physiologist John Sydney Edkins took a stance similar to Winchell's: "The teaching methods of the Edinburgh school involve both conciseness and dogmatism, and these are as desirable in elementary instruction as they are pernicious in more advanced."[40] In the same volume, another book reviewer also tried to reach a balanced judgment: "Used in its proper place, with students who have been well trained in general experimental science, and under the supervision of a capable teacher, there is no reason to suppose that the somewhat dogmatic statement of chemical laws will have

---

[37] [Alexander Winchell], "Thoughts on Science-Teaching," *Fortnightly Index* 31 (1884): 6–8, at 7. The essay was reprinted in Winchell's *Shall We Teach Geology? A Discussion of the Proper Place of Geology in Modern Education* (Chicago: S. C. Griggs and Company, 1889), 200–9.

[38] [H. E. Armstrong], "Scientific Education and Research," *Nature* 50, no. 1287 (1894): 211–14, at 212; Philip J. Hartog, "The Berthollet-Proust Controversy and the Law of Definite Proportions," *Nature* 50, no. 1285 (1894): 149–50, at 149; G. F. D., "Conferences of Mathematical Teachers and of Public School Science Masters," *Nature* 85, no. 2151 (1911): 385–6, at 386. See also "Letters to the Editor," *Nature* 80, no. 2058 (1909): 157–8, at 158.

[39] N. N., review of *Experimental Plant Physiology* by D. T. MacDougal, *Nature* 53, no. 1376 (1896): 436.

[40] J. S. Edkins, "Recent Works in Physiology," *Nature* 53, no. 1369 (1896): 266–7, at 266.

any ill result."[41] Apparently, there were different ways in which authors could try to reconcile the ideal of encouraging scientific thinking with the reality of inexperienced students needing plenty of instruction.

Similar observations can be made about nineteenth-century Germany. While some scholars preferred "genetic" over "dogmatic" modes of teaching,[42] others differentiated between the needs of students. The *Gymnasium* teacher and historian of physics Ferdinand Rosenberger, for example, argued that both "scholastic-dogmatic" and "historical-critical" methods had a place in the classroom. One argument for this position was that even the most critical researcher cannot do without a certain dose of dogmatism. More important, however, was Rosenberger's second argument. Students without academic aspirations, who are most likely going to find employment in "practical" jobs, will gain more useful knowledge from dogmatic expositions of scientific truths than from exercises in critical thinking. The reverse, however, is true for students who seek to become "masters of science" themselves. To cater to both groups, while stimulating independent work in both of them, teachers will need to "combine both methods."[43]

This argument, however, lost some of its appeal when educational theorists, inspired by Dewey and others, began to embrace the scientific "mindset," "spirit," or "attitude" as a means for socializing young people into a democratic ethos.[44] In their commitment to independent, critical thinking as a learning objective for students across the board, regardless of their vocational aspirations, early-twentieth-century educationalists became impatient with "those who hold exaggerated views of the need of dogmatic teaching for the young."[45] Some even deplored dogmatic teaching as the "tragedy of education." Edmond Holmes' 1913 book of that title included an entire chapter on "the poison of dogmatism," with "dogmatic teaching" serving as an umbrella term for educational drill, uninspired lecturing, and a spirit of reproduction rather than inquiry. (According to Holmes, even train passengers had to endure the tyranny of dogmatism, because they surrendered their freedom of choosing routes and departure times to "the dogmatic direction

[41] T., review of *Practical Proofs of Chemical Laws*, by Vaughan Cornish, *Nature* 53, no. 1359 (1895): 29.

[42] For example, Moritz Wilhelm Drobisch, *Neue Darstellung der Logik . . .*, 3rd ed. (Leipzig: Leopold Voss, 1863), 162; Hermann Kern, *Grundriss der Pädagogik*, 4th ed. (Berlin: Weidmann, 1887), 101.

[43] Ferd[inand] Rosenberger, "Die Geschichte der exakten Wissenschaften und der Nutzen ihres Studiums," *Abhandlungen zur Geschichte der Mathematik* 9 (1899): 359–81, at 375–6.

[44] On the subtle differences between these umbrella terms, see Andrew Jewett, *Science, Democracy, and the American University: From the Civil War to the Cold War* (Cambridge: Cambridge University Press, 2012), esp. 23–4, 41–3, 113–14.

[45] H. Macaulay Posnett, "A Word on Geological Hypothesis," *Geological Magazine* 7, no. 7 (1900): 298–302, at 301.

of the railway company.")[46] Such anti-dogmatic rhetoric left little room for the idea that dogmatic textbooks could be of use in the classroom.[47] Insofar as twentieth-century authors continued to defend dogmatic teaching, they mostly framed it in a Kuhn-like manner as a sociological necessity ("dogmatism is often unavoidable when brevity is sought") rather than as a cause worth striving for.[48]

*   *   *

Apparently, in the period under discussion, non-pejorative notions of dogmatism did not pose much of a challenge to the established view that dogmatism amounts to a scholarly vice. Even though such alternatives were repeatedly suggested, by prominent philosophers as well as by educational thinkers with first-hand knowledge of classroom realities, they were rejected again and again by critics for whom dogmatism had nothing but negative connotations. Telling in this regard is the fact that Kuhn felt compelled to give up the word—just as Francis Crick, a little later, apologized for his confusing concept of a "central dogma" in biology.[49] From a historical point of view, one might say that one seventeenth-century concept—the "vanity of dogmatizing" as thematized by Joseph Glanvill—had become entrenched so deeply in the scientific imagination that there was little room for retrievals of other early modern notions.

Insofar as dogmatic teaching nonetheless persisted, even into the twenty-first century, it did so *ex negativo*, as a danger that both scientists and educational thinkers continued to fight. Illustrative of this is a 2001 article on "the dogmatic teaching of ecology" that presents dogmatic teaching as a danger to scientific integrity. It approvingly quotes Popper while referring dismissingly to Kuhn. Also, it depicts dogmatism as an attitude typical of old-fashioned religion, which as such is out of place in modern science, while presenting its wisdom in a normative key ("we believe that dogmatic teaching of science is not advisable"). Consequently, the article exhorts its readers to practice virtues of rational, critical, undogmatic thinking.[50] Apparently, insofar as dogmatic teaching survives as a topic of debate in an anti-dogmatic intellectual climate, it does so as a bête noire, rhetorically invoked as a threat to highlight the importance of independent, critical thinking.

---

[46] Edmond Holmes, *The Tragedy of Education* (London: Constable & Company, 1913), 1–35, esp. 30.
[47] See, for example, Herbert R. Smith, review of *Chemistry Workbook and Laboratory Guide*, by M. V. McGill, *Journal of Chemical Education* 9, no. 1 (1932): 193–4, at 193.
[48] N. W. Pirie, review of *The Life Science* by P. B. and J. S. Medawar, *The New Scientist* 73, no. 1041 (1977): 537–8, at 537.
[49] As discussed in the Introduction.
[50] Rafael González Del Solar and Luis Marone, "The 'Freezing' of Science: Consequences of the Dogmatic Teaching of Ecology," *BioScience* 51, no. 8 (2001): 683–6, at 683.

7

The Dogmatic Personality

Psychological Research in Cold War America

If the influence of John Dewey and his progressive educational views was already palpable in early twentieth-century debates over dogmatic teaching, it became even more powerful in the aftermath of the Second World War. As argued in the previous chapter, it was this influence that contributed to Kuhn's thoughts on dogmatism falling on deaf ears in the early 1960s. Arguably, however, critical, scientific, reflective thinking as propagated by Dewey and like-minded educational thinkers had a more far-reaching impact on the history of dogmatism. As Andrew Jewett has pointed out, Dewey was a key representative of an intellectual tradition known as "scientific democracy."[1] At the heart of this tradition was the belief that scientific methods were beneficial to democratic societies insofar as they socialized citizens into virtues of critical thinking, independent judgment, and open-mindedness. When the atrocities of the Second World War and the onset of the Cold War prompted the emergence of "totalitarianism" as an umbrella category for both left- and right-wing authoritarian regimes, this belief turned into an article of faith for many self-declared guardians of democracy. As Jamie Cohen-Cole has shown, the virtue of open-mindedness together with its negative counterpart, the vice of dogmatism or closed-mindedness, acquired a prominent place in the American Cold War imagination.[2] If "closed" societies, governed by

---

[1] Andrew Jewett, *Science, Democracy, and the American University: From the Civil War to the Cold War* (Cambridge: Cambridge University Press, 2012).
[2] Jamie Cohen-Cole, *The Open Mind: Cold War Politics and the Sciences of Human Nature* (Chicago: University of Chicago Press, 2014), esp. 35–62.

authoritarian leaders and totalitarian ideologies, were perceived as dogmatic in the sense of requiring strict adherence to unquestionable truths, "open" societies were supposed to foster "open selves," adorned with the scientific-cum-political virtues that Dewey and his followers had been advocating since the 1910s.[3]

This chapter will examine how American psychologists in this strained Cold War context inaugurated a new phase in the history of dogmatism by developing scientific tools for measuring and diagnosing it. If dogmatism had so far been largely an academic invective, employed against non-academic actors only insofar as these were perceived as obstructing the free pursuit of science, it now became a research subject and the topic of a quickly growing pile of scientific studies. Even in this new context, however, scientists remained critical of dogmatic reasoning, while also continuing the nineteenth-century habit of attributing dogmatism to religious and political minorities (Catholics, communists). New elements thus mingled with older ones, thereby offering yet another glimpse into the entanglement of continuity and discontinuity in the history of dogmatism.

This chapter tells a story in three parts. First, it describes how Milton Rokeach proposed dogmatism or closed-mindedness as a conceptual alternative to "authoritarianism" such as used in *The Authoritarian Personality* (1950) by Theodor Adorno et alia. The chapter continues with a survey of the enormous success of Rokeach's dogmatism scale—a tool that purportedly enabled psychologists not only to diagnose dogmatism but also to examine its correlations with other psychological and developmental variables. (For instance, did "high" and "low" dogmatists respond differently to new products in the supermarket?) Finally, to illustrate some of the real-life effects of this dogmatism research, the chapter zooms in on one of Rokeach's graduate students, the psychologist C. Gratton Kemp, who helped cement the idea that closed-mindedness is antithetical to critical thinking. It shows that Rokeach's legacy lived on until well after his death in 1988, most notably among political psychologists and teachers of critical thinking skills.

*   *   *

The story starts in Berkeley, where Theodor Adorno, the exiled Frankfurt School philosopher, together with social psychologists Else Frenkel-Brunswik, Daniel Levinson, and Nevitt Sanford, worked for years on a book that eventually

---

[3] See, most notably, K. R. Popper, *The Open Society and Its Enemies*, vol. 1 (London: George Routledge & Sons, 1945). "Open selves" was a term coined by the American philosopher Charles Morris in *The Open Self* (New York: Prentice-Hall, 1948). See also Robert Oppenheimer, "The Open Mind: Prospects for World Peace," *Bulletin of the Atomic Scientists* 5, no. 1 (1949): 304–6.

appeared as *The Authoritarian Personality* (1950).[4] Although this almost 1,000-page study of the psychology of fascism was instantly welcomed as a "classic" and a "milestone," it also raised many an eyebrow, mainly because of its eclectic combination of empirical psychological research and Marxist–Freudian theory. At a time when American psychologists tried to turn their field into a rigorous branch of science, critics found themselves unhappy with the book's unrepresentative samples, unvalidated questionnaires, and "mere statements of opinion" posing as data analysis.[5] At the same time, critical theorists had reason to wonder why Adorno had collaborated with positivist-inclined social scientists, given that the Frankfurt School had always treated positivism as another wicked manifestation of the same modernity that had produced fascism. The ties between modernity and fascism, moreover, also divided contributors. While Adorno regarded "the authoritarian personality" as an individual manifestation of a societal pathology, his American colleagues preferred to locate the problem in the individual rather than in society at large, thereby leaving open the possibility of a non-fascist modernity.[6] Although *The Authoritarian Personality* was hugely influential—as early as 1954, a survey article referred to "scores of doctoral theses and hundreds of less elaborate studies which have used its concepts and its tests"—this was partly because the study's in-built tensions raised more questions than they could answer.[7]

Relevant for our purposes is especially the tension between "fascism" (the right-wing-inspired forms of anti-Semitism with which Adorno and his colleagues were most concerned) and the book's more generic concept of "authoritarianism." In a widely noted essay, written at the height of the Cold War, sociologist Edward Shils raised the question of why left-wing authoritarianism had been left out of the picture.[8] Similar worries were voiced in circles of the American Jewish Committee, one of the main funders of *The Authoritarian Personality*. Hadn't Adorno and his co-authors targeted the wrong enemy?[9] Although Nevitt Sanford rejected this criticism as anachronistic—

[4] T. W. Adorno et al., *The Authoritarian Personality* (New York: Harper & Row, 1950).

[5] Herbert H. Hyman and Paul B. Sheatsley, "'The Authoritarian Personality': A Methodological Critique," in Richard Christie and Marie Jahoda (eds.), *Studies in the Scope and Method of "The Authoritarian Personality"* (Glenceo: Free Press, 1954), 50–122 (quote at 120).

[6] Peter E. Gordon, "Realism and Utopia in *The Authoritarian Personality*," *Polity* 54, no. 1 (2022): 8–28, esp. 11–16.

[7] Nathan Glazer, "New Light on 'the Authoritarian Personality': A Survey of Recent Research and Criticism," *Commentary* 17 (1954): 289–97, at 290.

[8] Edward A. Shils, "Authoritarianism: 'Right' and 'Left,'" in Christie and Jahoda, *Studies in the Scope and Method*, 24–49. See also H. J. Eysenck, *The Psychology of Politics* (London: Routledge & Kegan Paul, 1954), esp. 149.

[9] Franz Samelson, "The Authoritarian Personality from Berlin to Berkeley and Beyond: The Odyssey of a Problem," in William F. Stone, Gerda Lederer, and Richard Christie (eds.), *Strength and Weakness: The Authoritarian Personality Today* (New York: Springer, 1993), 22–43, at 37.

when research had started in 1943–4, there had been no communist threat on the horizon[10]—Adorno took it very seriously. Interpreting it as evidence of an emerging anti-communist witch hunt, he decided that he had better leave the United States and return to Germany.[11]

More sympathetic to Shils was psychologist Milton Rokeach, a former student of Frenkel-Brunswik and Sanford who would later claim that his youth among orthodox Jews and Marxists in Brooklyn had made him wary of dogmatism in all forms and shapes.[12] Whatever the truth of this story, Rokeach left no doubt as to where he stood vis-à-vis Shils' criticism of Adorno: "With this criticism we agree, except that it does not go far enough."[13] In a series of papers published in the 1950s, Rokeach developed the "dogmatic personality" as a conceptual alternative to the "authoritarian personality." What defined this dogmatic personality was not a left- or right-wing ideological commitment but a cognitive style that Rokeach claimed could be found among National-Socialists and Marxist-Leninists alike. This style was not "open" in Popper's sense of the word—critical, rational, independent—but "closed" in that it organized its beliefs about the world into relatively coherent systems, which were resistant to change to the extent that they were based on authority (a party, a church) rather than on independent inquiry. In Rokeach's more technical language, dogmatism thus amounted to "(a) a relatively closed cognitive organization of beliefs and disbeliefs about reality, (b) organized around a central set of beliefs about absolute authority which, in turn, (c) provides a framework for patterns of intolerance and qualified tolerance toward others."[14]

What this definition shows is that dogmatism for Rokeach was a concept like "totalitarianism" as used by Hannah Arendt and other political theorists in the 1950s: it was an umbrella category created to capture both left- and right-wing aberrations from what was regarded as the norm.[15] The difference, however, was that dogmatism was not merely a concept. Rokeach also wanted it to be a psychological tool, allowing for empirical research in an age of behavioral science. To that end, he developed a "dogmatism scale" that would allow psychologists to measure to what degree individuals were

---

[10] Nevitt Sanford, "The Approach to the Authoritarian Personality," in J. L. McCary (ed.), *Psychology of Personality: Six Modern Approaches* (New York: Logos Press, 1956), 253–319, at 264.

[11] Uta Gerhardt, "Worlds Come Apart: Systems Theory versus Critical Theory: Drama in the History of Sociology in the Twentieth Century," *The American Sociologist* 33, no. 2 (2002): 5–39, at 19.

[12] "Milton Rokeach's Acceptance," *Political Psychology* 10, no. 1 (1989): 195–6, at 195.

[13] Milton Rokeach, *The Open and Closed Mind: Investigations into the Nature of Belief Systems and Personality Systems* (New York: Basic Books, 1960), 13.

[14] Milton Rokeach, "The Nature and Meaning of Dogmatism," *Psychological Review* 61, no. 3 (1954): 194–204, at 195.

[15] On American understandings of "totalitarianism" at the time, see Benjamin L. Alpers, *Dictators, Democracy, and American Public Culture: Envisioning the Totalitarian Enemy, 1920s–1950s* (Chapel Hill: University of North Carolina Press, 2003), 250–302.

"dogmatic" or "closed-minded" (terms that Rokeach used interchangeably). The scale included items like the following, both of which were aimed at testing respondents' submission to authority:

14. In this complicated world of ours the only way we can know what's going on is to rely on leaders or experts who can be trusted.

17. There's no use wasting your money on newspapers which you know in advance is [*sic*] just plain propaganda.

Other items were related to belief in a political cause:

30. A man who does not believe in some great cause has not really lived.

36. In times like these, a person must be pretty selfish if he considers primarily his own happiness.

Perhaps most strikingly, the dogmatism scale also included a set of questions about "concern with power and status," which Rokeach interpreted as testifying to a "need for self-aggrandizement" that was as psychologically unhealthy as it was politically dangerous:

57. While I don't like to admit this even to myself, my secret ambition is to become a great man, like Einstein or Beethoven, or Shakespeare.

60. If I had to choose between happiness and greatness, I'd choose greatness.[16]

In the history of dogmatism, the publication of this "D scale" was an event of some significance. If "dogmatism" had always been used loosely, as a term of abuse that scholars could throw at each other without having to spell out in what sense or to what degree they perceived their opponents as dogmatic, Rokeach offered a tool for examining with statistical precision (complete with mean scores and standard deviations) to what extent respondents suffered from closed-mindedness. One may object, of course, that respondents were a different population than academic opponents and that Rokeach's scale expanded dogmatism's realm of application more than it affected scholars' habit of accusing each other of dogmatic inclinations. This, however, would underestimate the impact of Rokeach's intervention. As we shall see in a moment, Rokeach-style dogmatism would enter scholars' polemical arsenal, too.

* * *

---

[16] Milton Rokeach, "Political and Religious Dogmatism: An Alternative to the Authoritarian Personality," *Psychological Monographs: General and Applied* 70, no. 18 (1956): 1–43, at 8, 9.

The impact of Rokeach's dogmatism research, such as accessibly summarized in *The Open and Closed Mind* (1960), was largely due to the D scale. Just as American psychologists primarily remembered *The Authoritarian Personality* for its "fascism scale," so Rokeach became known for his dogmatism scale (especially in form E, which included a mere forty instead of sixty-six items). Although there was methodological criticism already at an earlier stage, the combined weight of which would lead Bob Altemeyer to complain that "the D Scale is an even bigger nightmare than the F scale,"[17] enthusiasm for its wide scope of application far outweighed technical worries about, for instance, Rokeach's unidirectional wording of scale items.[18] A 1969 survey published in the *Psychological Bulletin* listed more than a hundred studies that made use of the D scale.[19]

Psychologists working on personality traits, for instance, found that dogmatic persons were "impulsive, defensive, and conventional and stereotyped in thinking."[20] If they had to choose whom to believe—police officers or student rioters, each with their own version of what happened in the San Francisco City Hall Riots of May 1960—they would trust the police more than the students.[21] Also, Roman Catholics with high scores on the D scale appeared to be more critical of liturgical change than non-dogmatic churchgoers.[22] Upper-middle and top managers were found to be significantly less dogmatic than first-line or lower-middle managers, which suggested that dogmatism was not a great leadership quality.[23] A graduate student

---

[17] Bob Altemeyer, *Right-Wing Authoritarianism* (Winnipeg: University of Manitoba Press, 1981), 90.
[18] John P. Kirscht and Ronald C. Dillehay, *Dimensions of Authoritarianism: A Review of Research and Theory* (Lexington: University of Kentucky Press, 1967), 11.
[19] Ralph B. Vacchiano, Paul S. Strauss, and Leonard Hochman, "The Open and Closed Mind: A Review of Dogmatism," *Psychological Bulletin* 71, no. 4 (1969): 261–73. It is worth noting that Rokeach's research was also picked up by scholars in Europe. See, for example, Johannes C. Brengelmann and Leo Brengelmann, "Deutsche Validierung von Fragebogen dogmatischer und intoleranter Haltungen," *Zeitschrift für Experimentelle und Angewandte Psychologie* 7 (1960): 451–71; Christiane Schmerl and Helmut Bonn, "Zum Problem dogmatischer Einstellungen bei 'Rechten' und 'Linken,'" *Soziale Welt* 26, no. 2 (1975): 174–87; Suitbert Ertel's much-discussed article,"Überzeugung, Dogmatismus, Wahn," *Georgia Augusta* 24 (1976): 32–9; and Peter Keiler and Michael Stadtler (eds.), *Erkenntnis oder Dogmatismus? Kritik des "Dogmatismus"-Konzepts* (Cologne: Pahl-Rugenstein, 1978).
[20] Walter T. Plant, Charles W. Telford, and Joseph A. Thomas, "Some Personality Differences between Dogmatic and Nondogmatic Groups," *The Journal of Social Psychology* 67, no. 1 (1965): 67–75, at 75.
[21] John McCarthy and Ronald C. Johnson, "Interpretation of the 'City Hall Riots' as a Function of General Dogmatism," *Psychological Reports* 11, no. 1 (1962): 243–5.
[22] Gordon J. DiRenzo, "Dogmatism and Orientations towards Liturgical Change," *Journal for the Scientific Study of Religion* 6, no. 2 (1967): 278.
[23] M. John Close, "The Open Versus Closed Mind in Management: An Exploration" (PhD thesis, Louisiana State University, 1974).

of Rokeach, applying his teacher's work to musical preference, found that dogmatic respondents showed a greater appreciation for "traditional" pieces like Johannes Brahms' C Minor String Quartet than for the twelve-tone music of Arnold Schönberg's String Quartet No. 4.[24] Similarly, high scorers turned out to be less receptive to unconventional animation films (*Begone Dull Care*) and modern painting (Pablo Picasso, Wassily Kandinsky) than people with lower scores.[25] Somewhat surprisingly perhaps, high-dogmatic subjects were also shown to be more inclined to purchase new consumer goods than low-dogmatic respondents—a finding that was interpreted, not as evidence of curiosity or flexibility but as demonstrating that dogmatists obeyed the cultural authorities who told them that buying new stuff is good for the economy and, consequently, good for America.[26]

Politically more sensitive were studies of American perceptions of the Vietnam War. Independently of each other, several teams of psychologists found a positive correlation between dogmatism as measured by the D Scale and "hawkish" attitudes toward the war.[27] Similarly, psychologist Alexander Askenasy studied how well US Army officers stationed in South Korea were able to estimate Korean opinions on American foreign policy and military strategy. His conclusion: "Officers who were relatively more 'dogmatic' (as determined by Rokeach's Dogmatism Scale) were less accurate and tended to overestimate Korean anti-American opinions."[28] Obviously, such findings had potential real-life effects as they not only analyzed the cognitive abilities of American service members but also provided their superiors with a "scientific" personnel selection tool: overly dogmatic soldiers were better not promoted to military leadership positions.[29]

---

[24] Bernard Mikol, "Open and Closed Belief Systems as Correlates of the Acceptance of New Music and Its Composers" (PhD thesis, Michigan State University, 1958).

[25] Salvatore Zagona and Marynell Kelly, "The Resistance of the Closed Mind to a Novel and Complex Audio-Visual Experience," *The Journal of Social Psychology* 70, no. 1 (1966): 123–31; Robert M. Frumkin, "Sex, Familiarity, and Dogmatism as Factors in Painting Preferences," *Perceptual and Motor Skills* 17, no. 1 (1963): 12.

[26] Brian Blake, Robert Perloff, and Richard Heslin, "Dogmatism and Acceptance of New Products," *Journal of Marketing Research* 7, no. 4 (1970): 483–6, at 486, 484.

[27] Stuart A. Karabenich and R. Ward Wilson, "Dogmatism among War Hawks and Peace Doves," *Psychological Reports* 25, no. 2 (1969): 419–22; Daniel W. Bailes and Irving B. Guller, "Dogmatism and Attitudes Towards the Vietnam War," *Sociometry* 33, no. 2 (1970): 140–6; Donald Granberg and Gail Gorrigan, "Authoritarianism, Dogmatism and Orientations Toward the Vietnam War," *Sociometry* 35, no. 3 (1972): 468–76.

[28] Alexander R. Askenasy, *Perception of Korean Opinions: A Study of U.S. Army Officers' Expertise* (Washington, DC: Center for Research in Social Systems, 1969), viii.

[29] Application of Rokeach's work in the area of personnel selection was also recommended in Kathryn McCloud and Aline H. Kidd, "Rokeach's Dogmatism Scale in the Selection of Psychiatric Nursing Personnel," *Psychological Reports* 13, no. 1 (1963): 241–2.

The political sensitivity of Rokeach's D scale in a Cold War context is perhaps even more apparent from how *The Open and Closed Mind* was received in the emerging field of political psychology. In a glowing review of Rokeach's book, Ralph White from the United States Information Agency—a pro-American, anti-Soviet public relations organization run by the US government—came straight to the point:

> In our nuclear age there could hardly be a more important subject than this one. The threat of Communists to peace and to Western democracy is not inherent in the nature of "socialism"; it is inherent, perhaps, in the kind of black-and-white dogmatic thinking that seems to be ingrained in the minds of the decision-makers in Moscow and Peking. Nor is such thinking confined to their side of the Iron and Bamboo Curtains. On our side too there are dogmatists who equate black-and-white thinking with firmness, intolerance with strength, and reasonableness with appeasement.[30]

Clearly, the black-and-white thinkers "on our side" had more to fear from Rokeach's research than communist leaders in faraway Moscow or Peking. The D scale could be used to identify potential threats to national security: dogmatists who were insufficiently democratic, overly receptive to communist influence, or characterologically incapable of knowing their place. As long as dogmatism was a vice with political relevance, an amateur pianist who secretly dreamt of becoming a new Beethoven had better not be too honest in filling out Rokeach's forms.

*   *   *

By the 1960s, though, the political risks involved in being exposed as dogmatic had become much smaller than a decade before. American universities no longer fired faculty members suspected of communist sympathies, as the University of Washington had done in 1949. Likewise, the loyalty oaths that universities had demanded in the late 1940s and early 1950s had become things of the past.[31] Although anti-communist sentiments had certainly not faded, the militant language that had been customary among university administrators at the heyday of McCarthyism—"that a member of the

---

[30] Ralph K. White, "A Landmark in the Study of Unreason and Intolerance," *Merrill–Palmer Quarterly of Behavior and Development* 7, no. 2 (1961): 139–42, at 139.
[31] Ellen W. Schrecker, *No Ivory Tower: McCarthyism and the Universities* (New York: Oxford University Press, 1986), 84–125.

Communist Party is not a free man, that he is instead a slave to immutable dogma"—had softened significantly.[32]

Nonetheless, Rokeach's dogmatism research had an impact well beyond the discipline of psychology. This was perhaps most visible in the realm of learning, where educational theorists following in the footsteps of Dewey habitually contrasted "reflective" or "scientific" students with "uncritical" or "dogmatic" thinkers.[33] One of Rokeach's graduate students, C. Gratton Kemp, provided fresh input into this conversation by demonstrating that high dogmatists performed not nearly as well in critical thinking tests as low dogmatists. He explained this by hypothesizing that high scorers cannot bear uncertainty for more than a moment: they are "impelled toward a 'closure' before full consideration is given to each piece of contributing evidence."[34] This in turn implied that highly dogmatic students needed help. If teachers had "to unleash the mind of the dogmatic," as a mathematics teacher wrote in response to Kemp's findings, they had to understand "the conditions which could be expected to help the closed-minded."[35] Kemp himself suggested that small-scale, informal environments could help dogmatic individuals lower their defenses and spend more time analyzing problems in all their dimensions.[36] Others, by contrast, pointed out that there was only so much that teachers could do. In 1963, a longitudinal study carried out by Irvin Lehmann and Paul Dressel (with Rokeach on the advisory board) showed that college dropouts in Michigan developed undogmatic thinking habits to the same degree and at the same pace as their peers in college, which suggested that class attendance did not make much of a difference.[37] Still others, more convinced that interventions were needed, proposed special teaching modules or training sessions targeted at cultivating critical thinking skills, thereby launching a whole industry of educational products that by the 1980s would include VHS

---

[32] Raymond B. Allen, "Communists Should Not Teach in American Colleges," The Educational Forum 13, no. 4 (1949): 433–40, as quoted in Cohen-Cole, Open Mind, 53.

[33] Douglas J. Simson, "John Dewey's Concept of the Dogmatic Thinker: Implications for the Teacher," Journal of Philosophy and History of Education 49 (1999): 159–72.

[34] C. Gratton Kemp, "Effect of Dogmatism on Critical Thinking," Journal of School Science and Mathematics 60, no. 4 (1960): 314–19, at 318, literally repeated in "Critical Thinking: Open and Closed Minds," The American Behavioral Scientist 5, no. 5 (1962): 10–15, at 11.

[35] Philip Peak, "Have You Read?" The Mathematics Teacher 54, no. 1 (1961): 16; Kemp, "Critical Thinking," 15.

[36] Kemp, "Effect of Dogmatism," 319.

[37] Irvin J. Lehmann and Paul L. Dressel, Changes in Critical Thinking Ability, Attitudes, and Values Associated with College Attendance (East Lansing: Michigan State University, 1963), 49. See also, by the same authors, Critical Thinking, Attitudes, and Values in Higher Education (East Lansing: Michigan State University, 1962), 267.

video courses on "Critical Thinking in Science" and "The Attributes of a Critical Thinker."[38]

Rokeach's shadow loomed large over all this insofar as critical thinking continued to be contrasted with dogmatism or closed-mindedness. If dogmatism persisted anywhere, it was in the critical thinking movement as institutionalized in the United States from the early 1970s onward. In the 1980s, the movement's best-known representative, Richard Paul, wrote one piece after another explaining that critical thinking was needed to correct the widespread prejudice that "it is always the other guys who do evil, who are deceived, self-interested, closed-minded—never us."[39] Critical thinking had to confront people with their own closed-mindedness, teaching them that "open-mindedness may be the proper, but . . . not the 'natural', disposition of the human mind."[40] What this shows is that critical thinking was not only *justified* in terms of rampant dogmatism ("We live in a world of flagrant dogmatism")[41] but also carried the promise of a *remedy* to dogmatism. Students were not "condemned to closed-mindedness": they could develop a "free and open mind," if only they received proper critical thinking instruction.[42]

*   *   *

Does this warrant the conclusion that Rokeach and his fellow psychologists in Cold War America moved dogmatism out of the realm of accusatory rhetoric to transform it into both a scientific research subject and a policy concern for teachers committed to open societies? To some extent, this is, indeed, what happened. What was new in 1950s America, compared to earlier periods discussed in this book, was that "dogmatism" became a subject of scientific research. If the term used to be invoked as an invective in the heat of polemic, it now became a research tool, complete with validated survey scales. However, appearances notwithstanding, this did not imply that dogmatism lost its pejorative connotations. To the extent that psychological methods became the "methods by which the open society improves and corrects its existing institutions," as the philosopher William Morris argued in *The Open*

---

[38] *The Seventh Annual and Fifth International Conference on Critical Thinking and Educational Reform, August 2–5, 1987: Program and Abstracts* ([Rohnert Park]: Center for Critical Thinking and Moral Critique, [1987]), 10, 104.

[39] Richard W. Paul, "Ethics without Indoctrination," *Educational Leadership* 45, no. 8 (1988): 10–19, at 11.

[40] Richard W. Paul, "Critical Thinking: Fundamental to Education for a Free Society," *Educational Leadership* 42, no. 1 (1984): 4–14, at 7.

[41] Linda Elder and Richard Paul, "Critical Thinking: Why We Must Transform Our Teaching," *Journal of Developmental Education* 18, no. 1 (1994): 34–5, at 34.

[42] Paul, "Critical Thinking," 12.

Self,[43] they were driven by a normative view of what openness entailed. In practice, this meant that they were often used to draw attention to those segments of society that were not yet sufficiently open.

American Catholics, most notably, found themselves diagnosed in study after study as far more dogmatic than Protestants and Jews.[44] Although it was no longer bon ton to dismiss Catholicism as "the oldest and greatest totalitarian movement in history,"[45] these repeated charges of closed-mindedness prompted irritation and even a small wave of counter-research at the University of Notre Dame, where Catholic psychologists used Rokeach's D scale to show that only conservative or moralistic Catholics were guilty of excessive dogmatism.[46] In the context of the Second Vatican Council (1962–5) and its contested program of modernizing Catholic doctrine and practice, this finding had, of course, its own polemical subtext.

In the 1980s, the politics of studying closed-mindedness became even more explicit. When Richard Paul spoke about "closed-minded zealots eager to remake the world in their image," he was thinking of conservative politicians like Ronald Reagan.[47] Likewise, at a conference marking the twenty-fifth anniversary of *The Open and Closed Mind*, educational theorist Forrest Parkay argued that public schools had to be protected against an emerging New Right that he believed to consist of "zealots and extremists" exhibiting "a strong tendency toward authoritarian, dogmatic thinking" as defined by Adorno and Rokeach.[48] After the 1981 *Segraves v. State of California* case concerning the teaching of evolutionary biology in public schools, much the same happened to creationists (on whom more in Chapter 8). In this respect, there was nothing new under the sun: dogmatism continued to evoke the highest degree of emotion when the borders between science, politics, and religion were at stake.

---

[43] Morris, *Open Self*, 154.

[44] For example, Rokeach, *Open and Closed Mind*, 349–52; Lehmann and Dressel, *Critical Thinking*, 265; Emma M. Cappelluzzo and James Brine, "Dogmatism and Prospective Teachers," *Journal of Teacher Education* 20, no. 2 (1969): 148–52, at 151; Andrew D. Thompson, "Open-Mindedness and Indiscrimination Antireligious Orientation," *Journal for the Scientific Study of Religion* 13, no. 4 (1974): 471–7.

[45] Sidney Hook, *Reason, Social Myths, and Democracy* (New York: John Day, 1940), 76. Changing perceptions of American Catholicism are discussed in John T. McGreevy, "Thinking on One's Own: Catholicism in the American Intellectual Imagination, 1928–1960," *The Journal of American History* 84, no. 1 (1997): 97–131.

[46] Joseph J. Lengermann and William V. D'Antonio, "Religion, Dogmatism, and Community Leadership: An Extension of the Theories of The Open and Closed Mind," *Sociological Analysis* 25, no. 3 (1964): 141–58; Lawrence Hong, "Religious Styles, Dogmatism and Orientations to Change," *Sociology of Religion* 27, no. 4 (1966): 239–42.

[47] Paul, "Ethics Without Indoctrination," 11; "Critical Thinking," 8.

[48] Forrest W. Parkay, "The Authoritarian Assault upon the Public School Curriculum: An Additional 'Indicator of Risk,'" *The High School Journal* 68, no. 3 (1985): 120–8, at 120, 121.

8

Challenging Dogmas

From Character Vice to Theory Vice

What happened to "dogmatism"—its meanings, its functions, the repertoires from which the term was drawn—in the decades leading up to the present? Throughout this book, we have seen moments of discontinuity being entangled with lines of continuity. Despite dogmatism taking on new meanings and functions, old habits continued to make their impact felt. Even when dogmatism was turned into a racial stereotype, a political threat, or a personality trait that psychologists could diagnose with scientific tools, it continued to be a character vice with connotations of outdatedness and clerical authority. The recent past, from the 1960s to the present, is no exception to this pattern. Compared to earlier periods covered in this book, the late twentieth and early twenty-first centuries showed elements of continuity and change. In this case, however, there is reason to expect that the latter outweighed the former.

Late-twentieth-century science, after all, is often portrayed as inhospitable to notions of virtue and vice. Besides the fact that the words "virtue" and "vices" had become archaic and talk of "character" had long been replaced by idioms of "personality" and "attitudes,"[1] scholarship on the norms and values

---

[1] Andrew Jewett, *Science, Democracy, and the American University: From the Civil War to the Cold War* (Cambridge: Cambridge University Press, 2012); Warren I. Susman, "'Personality' and the Making of Twentieth-Century Culture," in John Higham and Paul K. Conkin (eds.), *New Directions in American Intellectual History* (Baltimore: Johns Hopkins University Press, 1979), 212–26; Rebecca B. Miller, "Making Scientific Americans: Identifying and Educating Future Scientists and Nonscientists in the Early Twentieth Century" (PhD thesis, Harvard University, 2017), 121–49.

of science had begun to privilege collective levels of analysis over the personal level of character traits. Robert Merton's influential account of the ethos of science, for example, focused on institutionalized standards of conduct to which individual virtues or vices were largely irrelevant.[2] In a 1968 book on the social dimensions of science, theoretical physicist John Ziman even went so far as to say that virtues and vices belonged to a bygone age of gentlemen scholars pursuing solitary research in a corner of their kitchens. In a time of laboratory teamwork, research workers no longer needed "angelic qualities of mind." What mattered was, rather, that they conformed to institutional norms, imposed on them by the scientific community. Accordingly, the pious admonitions of earlier generations ("Be honest, be truthful, be objective") could be replaced by more practical questions: "Have you checked for instrumental errors? Is that series convergent? Would anyone understand that sentence? What is the present status of that old bit of theory?"[3]

Given this shift of focus from the individual to the collective, it makes sense to focus this final chapter on the question: What happened to dogmatism in the classic sense of a scholarly vice? Our answer will be twofold. On the one hand, we will argue that dogmatism transformed from a character vice into a theory vice, that is, from a scholar's personal quality into a feature of a scientific theory. Clearly, this amounted to a break with the past. On the other hand, there were countertrends: old habits that persisted as well as new developments, such as the rise of virtue ethics and virtue epistemology. Hence, the picture emerging from this chapter will be ambivalent. While dogmatic theories replaced dogmatic scholars as a main topic of concern, there were fields and genres in which the vice of dogmatism maintained a privileged position or, after a period of relative neglect, moved to center stage again.

*   *   *

The first signs of a new era in the history of dogmatism became visible when Rokeach was still developing his dogmatism scale. One such sign was Noam Chomsky's 1959 review of B. F. Skinner's *Verbal Behavior*

---

[2] Robert K. Merton, "The Normative Structure of Science" (1942), in Merton, *The Sociology of Science: Theoretical and Empirical Investigations*, ed. Norman W. Storer (Chicago: University of Chicago Press, 1973), 267–78. On dogmatism as a Mertonian "counter-norm," see Ian I. Mitroff, "Norms and Counter-Norms in a Select Group of the Apollo Moon Scientists: A Case Study of the Ambivalence of Scientists," *American Sociological Review* 39, no. 4 (1974): 579–95, at 592.

[3] J. M. Ziman, *Public Knowledge: An Essay Concerning the Social Dimension of Science* (Cambridge: Cambridge University Press, 1968), 78, 79. As Steven Shapin points out, this line of reasoning met with criticism from authors who preferred not to see the individual scholar receding into the background: *The Scientific Life: A Moral History of a Late Modern Vocation* (Chicago: University of Chicago Press, 2008), 173–8.

(1957)—one the most notorious book reviews ever written by a linguist. To no small degree, this notoriety was caused by the piece's scathing tone. Chomsky minced no words in dismissing Skinner's behaviorist paradigm as dogmatic through and through.[4] When one of Skinner's students, in response to this review, said he would avoid "the provocation of an *ad hominem* reply," it was clear to whom this remark was addressed.[5] It might seem, then, as if Chomsky's outburst against Skinner continued a well-established tradition of academic vice-charging. At closer inspection, however, his accusations appear not to be targeted at Skinner himself but at his linguistic theories. Instead of contrasting the vice of dogmatism with virtues like open-mindedness, Chomsky distinguished between research of the sort conducted by himself and "dogmatic and perfectly arbitrary claims" of the kind made by Skinner.[6] Similarly, in a 1972 follow-up article, Chomsky argued that it was the behaviorist "claims" advanced by his opponent that deserved to be called "either dogmatic or uninteresting, depending on which interpretation we give to them." Accordingly, what Chomsky dismissed as "pure dogmatism" was not a *character vice* but a *theory vice* (a defect of his theory about the determining influence of environmental factors on linguistic behavior).[7]

How representative was this shift of focus from personal qualities to properties of theories? It is easy to invoke, by way of counterexample, some ad hominem polemics from around the same period. In the field of literary studies, for instance, F. R. Leavis, the grand old man of English literary criticism, was known as a man dogmatic to the bone: "His name is . . . a byword for dogmatic arrogance."[8] Leavis had earned this reputation because of his harsh style of criticizing and quasi-dictatorial leadership of a school of literary criticism that opponents liked to compare to "a religious or ideological sect."[9]

---

[4] Julie T. Andresen, "Skinner and Chomsky Thirty Years Later," *Historiographia Linguistica* 17, no. 1–2 (1990): 145–65, at 155; Javier Virués-Ortega, "The Case against B. F. Skinner 45 years Later: An Encounter with N. Chomsky," *The Behavior Analyst* 29, no. 2 (2006): 243–51, at 243–4.

[5] Kenneth MacCorquodale, "On Chomsky's Review of Skinner's *Verbal Behavior*," *Journal of the Experimental Analysis of Behavior* 13, no. 1 (1970): 83–99, at 84. For Skinner's own response, see "A Lecture on 'Having' a Poem," in B. F. Skinner, *Cumulative Record: A Selection of Papers*, 3rd ed. (New York: Appleton–Century–Crofts, 1972), 345–55.

[6] Noam Chomsky, review of *Verbal Behavior*, by B. F. Skinner, *Language* 35, no. 1 (1959): 26–58, at 43.

[7] Noam Chomsky, "Psychology and Ideology," *Cognition* 1, no. 1 (1972): 11–46, at 14. We coin the term "theory vice" in analogy to "theory virtue." On the latter, see Ernan McMullin, "The Virtues of a Good Theory," in Stathis Psillos and Martin Curd (eds.), *The Routledge Companion to Philosophy of Science* (London: Routledge, 2008), 498–508.

[8] Donald Davie, "British Criticism: The Necessity for Humility," in David H. Malone (ed.), *The Frontiers of Literary Criticism* (Los Angeles: Hennessey & Ingalls, 1974), 25–34, at 26.

[9] John Gross, *The Rise and Fall of the Man of Letters: Aspects of English Literary Life since 1800* (London: Weidenfeld and Nicolson, 1969), 281. On the strong emotions (antipathy as well as

Throughout the 1950s and 1960s, colleagues and former students complained about his "dogmatic sensitivity," "dogmatic valuations," "tone of dogmatism," or "narrow-mindedness, . . . rancor, and dogmatism."[10] While some of these critics applied the adjective specifically to Leavis' assertions as distinguished from his character,[11] "narrowness," "spitefulness," and "dogmatism" were more frequently understood as personal qualities.[12] Indeed, in the eyes of his critics, Leavis was an "arrogantly dogmatic, absolutist critic, behaving more like the Grand Inquisitor or Calvin than a sensible man of letters."[13] This Grand Inquisitor, however, does not seem particularly representative. In other fields of study at the time—biology, sociology, or linguistics—one searches in vain for Leavis-like epitomes of dogmatism. By the 1960s, "princes of dogmatism" as featured in Chapter 5 had become an extinguishing species.[14]

Scholarly book reviews show a similar picture. In its editorial guidelines, published in 1967, the journal *Contemporary Psychology* warned explicitly against vice-charging of the sort that had been customary in the nineteenth century: "Personal aspersions are taboo. Criticize the text, the ideas, the logic, the accuracy, not the author. Let all criticism be *ad verbum*, never *ad hominem*."[15] Obviously, the issuing of such instructions may reveal something about the persistence of old habits. Nonetheless, from about the

---

admiration) that Leavis' criticism elicited throughout the Commonwealth, see Christopher Hilliard, *English as a Vocation: The Scrutiny Movement* (Oxford: Oxford University Press, 2012).

[10] R. W. B. Lewis, review of *The Common Pursuit*, by F. R. Leavis, and *The Fields of Light*, by Reuben Arthur Brower, *The Hudson Review* 5, no. 2 (1952): 308–13, at 310; Bernard Heyl, "The Absolutism of F. R. Leavis," *The Journal of Aesthetics and Art Criticism* 13, no. 2 (1954): 249–55, at 253; Alexander Porteous, "The Strange Case of Dr Leavis and Mr Lawrence," *Quadrant* 6, no. 1 (1961): 11–22, at 12; Gabriel Gersh, "The Moral Imperatives of F. R. Leavis," *The Antioch Review* 28, no. 4 (1968): 520–8, at 522.

[11] For example, Heyl, "Absolutism," 253.

[12] Gross, *Rise and Fall*, 274. Cf. Peter Russell, "A Communication," *The Hudson Review* 5, no. 3 (1952): 460–4, at 462: "His bad manners have cut him off from the literary world, his vices have vitiated his virtues . . ."

[13] [J. B.] Priestley, "Thoughts on Dr. Leavis," *The New Statesman and Nation* 52, no. 1339 (1956): 579–80, at 580.

[14] This is not to deny, of course, that emotions between scholars could run high. Stephen Jay Gould's polemicizing against George Gaylord Simpson has even been described as father murder. Nonetheless, although Gould, commenting on *The Major Features of Evolution* (1953), claimed that "Simpson's text verges on the impatience of incipient dogmatism," Simpson did never become a "Mr. Dogmatism" in the way that Leavis did. Joe Cain, "Ritual Patricide: Why Stephen Jay Gould Assassinated George Gaylord Simpson," in David Sepkoski and Michael Ruse (eds.), *The Paleobiological Revolution: Essays on the Growth of Modern Paleontology* (Chicago: University of Chicago Press, 2009), 346–63, at 353; Stephen Jay Gould, "G. G. Simpson, Paleontology, and the Modern Synthesis," in Ernst Mayr and William B. Provine (eds.), *The Evolutionary Synthesis: Perspectives on the Unification of Biology* (Cambridge, MA: Harvard University Press, 1980), 153–72, at 167.

[15] E. G. Boring, "Comment to Reviewers," *Contemporary Psychology* 12, no. 8 (1967): 395–6. We owe this reference to Sjang ten Hagen.

1960s onward, we see the adjective "dogmatic" being applied to arguments and texts more than to their authors. Reviews in the *American Journal of Sociology* repeatedly refer to dogmatic definitions, assertions, and analyses, sometimes even to a dogmatic tone, but rarely to dogmatic character traits.[16] In *Science*, likewise, we find book reviewers pointing to dogmatic statements, assertions, interpretations, and answers—sometimes also to their absence in the publication under review—but never to an author's dogmatic habits or inclinations.[17] This ties in with recent findings on the use of virtue terms in postwar American science. Accuracy, carefulness, and objectivity were increasingly applied not to persons but to experiments, measurements, and analyses. They no longer denoted character virtues but described the accuracy, care, or objectivity with which research was being conducted or reported.[18]

Even in unlikely genres, such as criticism of Soviet scholarship in the heyday of the Cold War, a gradual shift in focus from character vices to theory vices can be discerned. Rokeach's dogmatic personality was, of course, an embodiment of vices. The D scale measured nothing but personality traits. Similarly, in 1951, Hans Ronimois—a Russian-born economist at the University of British Columbia whose bitter feelings over the Soviet takeover of his country of birth colored much of his writing—was implying vicious conduct when dismissing his Russian colleagues as "Soviet dogmatists" who uncritically "follow the Party line."[19] Ten years later, however, the philosopher Thomas Blakeley struck a different tone. "Western observers," he noticed, "are unanimous in characterizing contemporary Soviet philosophy as 'dogmatic.'" Blakeley deemed this a justified charge insofar as "the classics of Marxism-Leninism" served as courts of last resort in Soviet philosophical discourse.[20] This was not an observation about character traits but about standards of

---

[16] Bertell Ollman, review of *The Sociology of Marx*, by Henri Lefebvre, *American Journal of Sociology* 74, no. 4 (1969): 435–6, at 436; Pierre L. van den Berghe, review of *The New American Revolution*, by Roderick Aya and Norman Miller, *American Journal of Sociology* 77, no. 5 (1972): 981–2, at 981; Bernard S. Mayer and Thomas F. Mayer, review of *Rebellion, Revolution, and Armed Force*, by D. E. H. Russell, *American Journal of Sociology* 82, no. 2 (1976): 452–8, at 457. Both these references and those listed in the next footnote were provided by Sjang ten Hagen.

[17] J. T. Enright, "Responses to Light," *Science* 160, no. 3834 (1968): 1327–8, at 1328; E. Adamson Hoebel, "The Cultures and Evolution of the Indians," *Science* 165, no. 3890 (1969): 272–3, at 273; Arthur A. Spector, "Carbohydrates and Lipids," *Science* 186, no. 4166 (1974): 820; Peter Kareiva, "Community Ecology," *Science* 226, no. 4674 (1984): 532. See, however, by way of exception, Thomas P. Hughes, "The Space Agency as Manager," *Science* 157, no. 3794 (1967): 1298–9, at 1299.

[18] Kim M. Hajek, Herman Paul, and Sjang L. ten Hagen, "Objectivity, Honesty, and Integrity: How American Scientists Talked about Their Virtues, 1945–2000." *History of Science* (forthcoming).

[19] Hans E. Ronimois, "The Soviet Economic Machine," *The Slavonic and East European Review* 30, no. 74 (1951): 112–38, at 117.

[20] T. Blakeley, "Method in Soviet Philosophy," *Studies in Soviet Thought* 1 (1961): 17–28, at 17, 18.

philosophical reasoning.[21] Likewise, when American historians wrote about "dogmatic Marxism," "dogmatic Marxist treatment," and "dogmatic torpidity," they used these terms mainly to highlight the limitations of Marxist-inspired historiography, without pretending to offer anything like a Rokeachean analysis of the personalities behind it.[22]

So, even if these examples followed well-established patterns by invoking national stereotypes, turning a controversial scholar into a symbolic incarnation of vice, and using clichéd religious images, they illustrate that by the 1960s or 1970s the adjective "dogmatic" no longer self-evidently referred to scholars' character or personality traits. Although dogmatism as a character vice did not fall out of usage, the emergence of dogmatism as a theory vice is one of the more striking developments in this period.

* * *

To what extent can this same change be observed in controversies about sensitive topics? Earlier in this book, we noticed that charges of dogmatism often became more intense when scholars perceived the boundaries between science, politics, and religion to be at risk. A late-twentieth-century example of such a debate is the decades-long controversy provoked by the creationist movement. From the very start, charges of dogmatism flew back and forth between "creationists" and "evolutionists," mainly because all parties involved had strong opinions about teachers treating the book of Genesis as an alternative to *The Origins of Species*. Interestingly, it was the creationists who introduced the trope of dogmatism, as shorthand not for closed-mindedness but for monopolizing power. This is how Duane Gish, an American biochemist and founding member of the Institute for Creation Research, stated the problem in 1970:

> In all the history of science, never has dogmatism had such a firm grip on science as it does today with reference to evolution theory. Evolutionists control our schools, the universities, and the means of publication. It would be almost as surprising to find an antievolutionist holding an important

---

[21] Similarly, in Blakeley's book, *Soviet Scholasticism* (Dordrecht: D. Reidel, 1961), "scholasticism" denoted a quality of Soviet philosophical systems, not a personality trait of their adherents.

[22] Istvan Deak, review of *Kelet-Európa története a 19. század elsö felében*, by Endre Arató, *The American Historical Review* 79, no. 1 (1974): 186–7, at 186; John B. Wolf, review of *Fureurs paysannes*, by Roland Mousnier, *The American Historical Review* 74, no. 3 (1969): 947–8, at 947; and Robert V. Allen, *Wissenschaft in kommunistischen Ländern*, by Dietrich Geyer, *The American Historical Review* 74, no. 5 (1969): 1609–10, at 1609. We owe these references to Sjang ten Hagen.

professorship at one of our major universities as it would be to find a capitalist occupying a chair at Moscow University.[23]

It was this kind of argument, put forward time and again by the Institute for Creation Research, that led the California State Board of Education in 1972 to adopt a so-called "anti-dogmatism policy," according to which the origins of life should be taught in public schools, not as an issue settled by science or religion but as a matter of hypothesis. This anti-dogmatism policy was widely regarded as a victory for the creationist camp, as it required biology teachers to tell their students about alternatives to evolution theory.[24]

While "dogmatism" made it into policy documents, the term was used even more widely in polemical pieces, both by critics of the Californian resolution and by creationists pleading their case in scientific terms. Echoing nineteenth-century science and religion debates, both parties drew on ecclesial metaphors ("creeds," "high priests") to highlight their opponents' "politico-religious dogmatism."[25] When creationists found themselves accused of a lack of open-mindedness,[26] they themselves invoked the same virtue in cautioning against precipitous acceptance of evolution theory.[27] Critics of creationism also used dogmatism in a Popperian sense, as synonymous with non-falsifiability. According to paleontologist Stephen Jay Gould, "unbeatable systems are dogma, not science."[28] In 1982, philosopher Michael Ruse reached the same verdict in an article with the telling title "Creation Science: The Ultimate

---

[23] Duane T. Gish, "A Challenge to Neo-Darwinism," *The American Biology Teacher* 32, no. 8 (1970): 495–7, at 495.

[24] The story is told in detail in Edward J. Larson, *Trial and Error: The American Controversy over Creation and Evolution*, 3rd ed. (Oxford: Oxford University Press, 2003), 125–55 and Dorothy Nelkin, *Science Textbook Controversies and the Politics of Equal Time* (Cambridge, MA: MIT Press, 1977), 94–101.

[25] For example, Randy L. Wysong, *The Creation-Evolution Controversy* (Midland: Inquiry Press, 1976), 57, 419; N. N., "Unreason Threatens the Biological Synthesis," *The New Scientist* 91, no. 1269 (1981): 579. See also Bonnie L. Dwyer, "California Science Textbook Controversy," *Origins* 1, no. 1 (1974): 29–34, at 31.

[26] For example, Philip Kitcher, *Abusing Science: The Case against Creationism* (Cambridge, MA: MIT Press, 1982), 167–78.

[27] Until as late as 2001, public school biology textbooks in Alabama included a warning label that stated: "No one was present when life first appeared on earth. Therefore, any statement about life's origins should be considered as theory, not fact." This message was followed by the advice to "study hard and keep an open mind" so as not to become a dogmatic evolutionist. A reproduction can be found in Ronald L. Numbers, *The Creationists: From Scientific Creationism to Intelligent Design*, 2nd ed. (Cambridge, MA: Harvard University Press, 2006), 3. On the empiricist assumptions underlying this kind of discourse, see Charles Alan Taylor, *Defining Science: A Rhetoric of Demarcation* (Madison: University of Wisconsin Press, 1996), 143–57.

[28] Stephen Jay Gould, "Evolution as Fact and Theory," *Discover* 2, no. 5 (1981): 34–7, at 35.

Fraud": "Creation science is not science. It is crude dogmatic religion. For this reason, it is as offensive to the true believer as it is to the scientist."[29]

With emotions often running high, it is perhaps not surprising that attacks sometimes became personal, with ad hominem accusations being issued or implied. When Gould called creationists "a fanatical and dogmatic lot"[30] and Ruse accused them of lacking "the openness expected of scientists,"[31] they clearly were talking about character vices. Such personal vice-charging, however, also met with criticism, even from kindred spirits. Philosopher of science Larry Laudan, most notably, urged his fellow critics of creationism to keep their arguments impersonal. "The *ad hominem* charge of dogmatism against Creationism egregiously confuses doctrines with the proponents of those doctrines," Laudan explained in 1982. "What counts is the epistemic status of Creationism, not the cognitive idiosyncrasies of the creationists."[32] Obviously, there would have been no need for such counsel without scholars engaging in less subtle forms of criticism. Nonetheless, Laudan's reluctance to speak about character vices—"We can assess the merits or demerits of creationist theory without having to speculate about the unsavoriness of the mental habits of creationists"—was more than an individual preference.[33] It showed a commitment to evaluating research findings rather than the people behind them that we encountered earlier in Ziman, in Chomsky, and in the editorial guidelines of *Contemporary Psychology*.

*   *   *

Another body of evidence testifying to the gradual ascendency of dogmatism as a theory vice consists of journal articles featuring the word "dogma" or "dogmas" in their titles. When recent medical articles carry a subtitle like "Replacing Dogma with Data," it is obvious that they are referring not to character vices but to the power of medical dogma in the doctor's

---

[29] Michael Ruse, "Creation Science: The Ultimate Fraud," *The New Scientist* 94, no. 1307 (1982): 586–91, at 591. See also Ruse's review of *Abusing Science*, by Philip Kitcher, *Philosophy of Science* 51, no. 2 (1984): 348–54, at 348 ("crude, dogmatic, Biblical literalism, masquerading as genuine science").

[30] Stephen Jay Gould, "Creationism: Genesis vs. Geology," in Alan Dundes (ed.), *The Flood Myth* (Berkeley: University of California Press, 1988), 427–37, at 430. This article originally appeared in *The Atlantic* 250, no. 3 (1982): 10–17.

[31] Michael Ruse, "Response to the Commentary: Pro Judice," *Science, Technology, and Human Values* 7, no. 41 (1982): 19–23, at 23.

[32] Larry Laudan, "Commentary: Science at the Bar: Causes for Concern," *Science, Technology, and Human Values* 7, no. 41 (1982): 16–19, at 17.

[33] Larry Laudan, "More on Creationism," *Science, Technology, and Human Values* 8, no. 1 (1983): 36–8, at 37.

consulting room. What they seek to challenge are things like standard criteria for diagnosing vascular dementia and the reigning paradigm of hormone replacement theory.[34] Interestingly, this practice of conveying in a few catchy title words that conventional views or established theories ("dogmas") must be abandoned when new evidence renders them obsolete goes back to the early postwar period. From the 1950s onward, but with a significant increase near and after the turn of the century, we find journal article titles with standardized formulae ("challenging the dogma of . . .") expressing dissatisfaction with reigning dogmas, understood not as character vices but as theory vices.

W. V. Quine's 1951 essay, "Two Dogmas of Empiricism," is a case in point. This famous article attacked two classic philosophical ideas: the distinction between analytical and synthetic truths and the notion that all meaningful language can be reduced to empirical statements. What matters for our purposes is not what these ideas entailed but the way in which Quine presented them: as "dogmas" that were "ill founded" and, as such, a matter of "faith" rather than reason.[35] If Quine's argument struck a chord among philosophers,[36] his title, too, became a minor classic and subject to endless variation. Philosophers proposed "a third dogma of empiricism," while questioning "two dogmas of methodology."[37] Scholars in other disciplines followed with "two dogmas of liberalism," "two dogmas of charged particle optics," "two dogmas of curriculum," and "two dogmas of educational research" (followed by a "third dogma of educational research"). If one researcher wrote a critical piece on "two dogmas of computationalism," another managed to identify "three dogmas of materialist pragmatism" or launch an attack on the "four dogmas of environmental economics." After the turn of the twenty-first century, this game became so popular that new versions were produced on an annual basis. While philosophers pondered the "two dogmas" of belief revision, Davidsonian semantics, and Sartrean existentialism, others penned programmatic pieces on the "two dogmas" of consciousness, biology, neoclassical economics, discourse analysis, and research ethics. Scholars warned against the "three dogmas" of desire,

---

[34] John V. Bowler and Vladimir Hachinski, "Criteria for Vascular Dementia: Replacing Dogma with Data," *Archives of Neurology* 57, no. 2 (2000): 170–1; David M. Herrington, "Hormone Replacement Therapy and Heart Disease: Replacing Dogma with Data," *Circulation* 107, no. 1 (2003): 2–4.

[35] W. V. Quine, "Two Dogmas of Empiricism," *The Philosophical Review* 60, no. 1 (1951): 20–43, at 20, 34.

[36] John H. Zammito, *A Nice Derangement of Epistemes: Post-Positivism in the Study of Science from Quine to Latour* (Chicago: University of Chicago Press, 2004).

[37] In "Two Dogmas of Quineanism," *The Philosophical Review* 29, no. 117 (1979): 289–301, Graham Priest applied the metaphor to Quine's own work.

political theory, and intellectual property jurisprudence, while also drawing critical attention to the "four dogmas of linguisticism." The uncrowned king of the genre was, no doubt, the biologist Rupert Sheldrake, who in his popular book *Science Set Free* (2012) identified no less than "ten dogmas of modern science."[38]

What did all this dogma talk refer to? Insofar as authors commented on their choice of terminology, they explained that dogmas were ideas that were not "cogently argued for" or "convincedly established."[39] As "deeply entrenched assumptions," dogmas were said to be "often uncritically accepted," "seldom recognized," and "almost never challenged."[40] Some of these definitions echoed nineteenth-century connotations of outdatedness (Chapter 3). Medical ethicist Terrence Ackerman, for example, spoke about "traditional dogmas," while Sheldrake referred to "centuries-old assumptions that have hardened into dogmas."[41] Religious images as discussed in Chapter 4 also returned insofar as dogmas were equated with "orthodox theses," "articles of faith," or "creeds" that "most scientists take for granted."[42] The difference, however, was that nineteenth-century scholars had understood dogmatism as a character vice, whereas twentieth-century authors were most concerned about the power of dogmatic theories.

Something similar applies to other formulaic expressions, such as "challenging the dogma of . . ." When the dogma in question was as specific as "the dogma of mitochondrial reactive oxygen species overproduction in diabetic kidney disease," held by specialists in the field "for more than a decade," it looks as if the term could denote any piece of accepted wisdom that did not hold in light of new research.[43] This is confirmed by articles that set out to challenge the dogma of traumatic cardiac arrest management, high target doses in the treatment of heart failure, or colorectal peritoneal metastases as an untreatable condition. The point of calling an established

---

[38] Rupert Sheldrake, *Science Set Free: Ten Paths to New Discovery* (New York: Deepak Chopra, 2012), 6.

[39] Larry Laudan, "Two Dogmas of Methodology," *Philosophy of Science* 43, no. 4 (1976): 585–97, at 585.

[40] Mark Rowlands, "Two Dogmas of Consciousness," *Journal of Consciousness Studies* 9, nos. 5–6 (2002): 158–80, at 158; Max Kölbel, "Two Dogmas of Davidsonian Semantics," *The Journal of Philosophy* 98, no. 12 (2001): 613–35, at 614; Jane Roland Martin, "Two Dogmas of Curriculum," *Synthese* 51 (1982): 5–20, at 5.

[41] Terrence F. Ackerman, "Medical Ethics and the Two Dogmas of Liberalism," *Theoretical Medicine* 5 (1984): 69–81, at 70, 76; Sheldrake, *Science Set Free*, 6.

[42] Oron Shagrir, "Two Dogmas of Computationalism," *Minds and Machines* 7 (1997): 321–44, at 321; Sheldrake, *Science Set Free*, 7.

[43] Melinda T. Coughlan and Kumar Sharma, "Challenging the Dogma of Mitochondrial Reactive Oxygen Species Overproduction in Diabetic Kidney Disease," *Kidney International* 90, no. 2 (2016): 272–9, at 272.

theory a "prevailing dogma" was not to accuse its adherents of dogmatism but to say that its "assumption has been challenged by a growing body of evidence."[44] In all of these cases, dogma simply served as a pejorative label for theories or treatment protocols that new findings proved to be no longer tenable.

What this suggests is that philosopher Matthew Eshleman, writing in 2002, was wrong to suggest that "contesting dogma is often met with great alarm."[45] If dogmas are defined as unfounded assumptions that are misleading and harmful to the progress of science,[46] leaving them unchallenged is much worse than criticizing them.[47] Especially in contexts committed to innovation—that modern-day equivalent to nineteenth-century progress—challenging dogmas is what scholars are expected to do. As two computer scientists put it: "A scientist should be aware of the prevailing dogmas of his or her discipline, not only because dogmas misguide scientists but also because scientists need to refute existing dogmas to gain new understandings."[48]

* * *

Finally, if this trend identified in this chapter amounts to a gradual shift of focus from character vices to theory vices, how does the critical thinking movement as discussed near the end of Chapter 7 fit into the picture? Unlike the scientists featured in the present chapter, Richard Paul *cum suis* were not particularly interested in falsifying dogmas. As they were committed to cultivating critical, independent thinking in a Deweyan sense of the word, they focused their attention on the "disposition of the human mind" with an eye to helping students overcome the vice of closed-mindedness (Chapter 7).

---

[44] Yoshitoshi Ogura et al., "TccP2 of O157:H7 and Non-O157 Enterohemorrhagic *Escherichia coli* (EHEC): Challenging the Dogma of EHEC-Induced Actin Polymerization," *Infection and Immunity* 75, no. 2 (2007): 604–12, at 611; Philip M. Farrell, Elinor Langfelder-Schwind, and Michael H. Farrell, "Challenging the Dogma of the Healthy Heterozygote: Implications for Newborn Screening Policies and Practices," *Molecular Genetics and Metabolism* 134, nos. 1–2 (2021): 8–19, at 8.

[45] Matthew Eshleman, "Two Dogmas of Sartrean Existentialism," *Philosophy Today* 46, suppl. 9 (2002): 68–74, at 68.

[46] Alex John London, "Two Dogmas of Research Ethics and the Integrative Approach to Human-Subjects Research," *The Journal of Medicine and Philosophy* 32, no. 2 (2007): 99–116, at 100; Eric Grillo, "Two Dogmas of Discourse Analysis," in Grillo (ed.), *Power Without Domination: Dialogism and the Empowering Property of Communication* (Amsterdam: John Benjamins, 2005), 1–41, at 5; Amir Askari, "The Sodium Pump and Digitalis Drugs: Dogmas and Fallacies," *Pharmacology Research and Perspectives* 7, no. 4 (2019): e00505, 4.

[47] Cf. Alvin M. Weinberg, "The Axiology of Science," *American Scientist* 58, no. 6 (1970): 612–17, at 615: "Paradigm breaking is better than spectroscopy [i.e., adding details to an existing paradigm]."

[48] Teppo Eskelinen and Matti Tedre, "Three Dogmas of Computing" (2006), online at https://dokument.pub/three-dogmas-of-computing-joensuu-flipbook-pdf.html (accessed May 17, 2023).

Arguably, this interest in learners' character virtues and vices set the critical thinking movement somewhat apart from the main trend in this period. Insofar as it insisted on the need for students to become "a fundamentally open and undogmatic person," it continued an older strand of thinking instead of joining a new one—even though a book title like *How Dogmatic Beliefs Harm Creativity and Higher-Level Thinking* (2012) shows that the adjective "dogmatic" was not exclusively applied to character traits.[49]

If the critical thinking movement amounted to a countertrend, this is even more true of two other phenomena that the late twentieth century saw emerge: virtue ethics and virtue epistemology.[50] Born out of frustration with the dominance of Kantianism and utilitarianism in Anglo-American philosophy, both prompted a great deal of reflection on the importance of virtues, also for the pursuit of academic work. Although vices did not nearly receive the same amount of attention as virtues, they were, nonetheless, almost routinely invoked as negative counterparts of character traits that scholars must possess to do their work with integrity. Along these lines, the American philosopher James Montmarquet presented the dogmatist (personified as "Dan the Dogmatist"—a fictive character instead of a real-life prince) as a countermodel to a veracious, open-minded, intellectually humble inquirer.[51] Other philosophers followed suit with warnings against related ills such as closed-mindedness and "bullshit."[52] The early twenty-first century even saw some attempts to establish a subfield called vice epistemology, in which dogmatism features as a prime example of an intellectual habit that people should avoid if they care about democracy, peace, or the future of the planet.[53] Importantly, in all of this literature, the "*un*virtuous dogmatist" is criticized

---

[49] Nancy A. Stanlick and Michael J. Strawser, *Asking Good Questions: Case Studies in Ethics and Critical Thinking* (Indianapolis: Hackett, 2015), 81; Don Ambrose and Robert J. Sternberg (eds.), *How Dogmatic Beliefs Harm Creativity and Higher-Level Thinking* (New York: Routledge, 2012).

[50] Political psychology as practiced by Judy Johnson may also qualify as a countertrend insofar as it sought to alert citizens in an age of global warming and terrorist threats against "dogmatists who knowingly intensify our fears in such a way that we close our minds to reasonable alternatives." Judy J. Johnson, *What's So Wrong with Being Absolutely Right: The Dangerous Nature of Dogmatic Belief* (Amherst: Prometheus, 2009), 18–19. Johnson even devoted a novel to the dangers of dogmatism: *Thief of Reason* (Toronto: Iguana, 2021).

[51] James A. Montmarquet, "Epistemic Virtue," *Mind* 96, no. 384 (1987): 482–97, at 492, 485. See also Montmarquet, "Justification: Ethical and Epistemic," *Metaphilosophy* 18, nos. 3–4 (1987): 186–99, at 189.

[52] For example, Wayne Riggs, "Open-Mindedness," *Metaphilosophy* 41, nos. 1–2 (2010): 172–88; Heather Battaly, "Closed-Mindedness and Dogmatism," *Episteme* 15, no. 3 (2018): 261–82; Chris Heffer, "Bullshit and Dogmatism: A Discourse Analytical Perspective," in Alessandra Tanesini and Michael P. Lynch (eds.), *Polarisation, Arrogance, and Dogmatism: Philosophical Perspectives* (London: Routledge, 2021), 120–37.

[53] Quassim Cassam, *Vices of the Mind: From the Intellectual to the Political* (Oxford: Oxford University Press, 2019), 100–20; Alessandra Tanesini, *The Mismeasurement of the Self: A Study in Vice Epistemology* (Oxford: Oxford University Press, 2021), esp. 164–7.

not for the dogmatic nature of her beliefs but for character traits that are detrimental to the pursuit of knowledge.[54] Dogmatism, accordingly, is seen as "a property of people, not of beliefs."[55]

In light of these countertrends and the persistence of old habits, most notably in the creationist controversy, this chapter must conclude on a balanced note. The late twentieth and early twenty-first centuries clearly witnessed a growing unease with ad hominem polemics, which made character vices appear as less appropriate categories of analysis than theory vices.[56] This trend is reflected in a shift of focus from dogmatism as a scholarly vice to dogmas as well-entrenched beliefs obstructing the progress of science or the implementation of new evidence-based treatment protocols. If these developments point to what the title of this chapter calls a shift "from character vice to theory vice," it would be wrong, nonetheless, to reduce the story to a secessionist narrative of dogmas taking the place formerly occupied by dogmatism. Whenever students immerse themselves in critical thinking, virtue ethics, or virtue epistemology, they will be warned against dogmatism in the sense of a character vice that hampers the pursuit of scholarly goals. Although these countertrends hardly affect scientists' "dogma vs. data" rhetoric, they do make an impact in the educational sphere. One of the world's most widely used biomedical textbooks unequivocally tells its readers that dogmatic self-confidence is detrimental to research integrity.[57] Apparently, even in an age preoccupied with challenging dogmas, the vice of dogmatism—that legacy from seventeenth-century England that dominated so much of the story told in this book—persists as a relevant category for scholars concerned about the integrity of their profession.

---

[54] Montmarquet, "Epistemic Virtue," 487.

[55] Robert C. Roberts and W. Jay Wood, *Intellectual Virtues: An Essay in Regulative Epistemology* (Oxford: Clarendon Press, 2007), 194.

[56] Interestingly, some virtue epistemologists seem prepared to rehabilitate ad hominem reasoning, arguing that the modern aversion to it is rooted in an unconvincingly impersonal paradigm of scientific rationality: Christopher M. Johnson, "Reconsidering the *Ad Hominem*," *Philosophy* 84, no. 328 (2009): 251–66; Heather Battaly, "Attacking Character: Ad Hominem Argument and Virtue Epistemology," *Informal Logic* 30, no. 4 (2010): 361–90.

[57] Tom L. Beauchamp and James F. Childress, *Principles of Biomedical Ethics*, 5th ed. (Oxford: Oxford University Press, 2001), 17, 36.

9

Conclusion

Why did "dogmatism" survive the passage of time? Why did the term persist in modern scholarly discourse, despite its meanings often changing over time, in response to changing challenges and circumstances? This book has tried to explain this continuity-in-discontinuity by examining the history of "dogmatism" at three levels: (1) the meanings attributed to the term, (2) the functions it fulfilled (for what purposes did people invoke the term?), and (3) the repertoires on which scholars drew in accusing others of dogmatism, or in warning against the threat that they believed dogmatism to pose to the integrity of science. In these concluding remarks, we will summarize our findings and identify some possible directions for follow-up research.

At the level of meaning, we have encountered many changes over time. Some of the larger ones include the emergence of "dogmatism" as a vice instead of a method, the increasingly archaic connotations that the term acquired, and the analogy with clerical authority expressed in metaphors like "popes," "creeds," and "infallible dogmas." We will return to these three major changes in a moment, as their impact on the history of dogmatism has been long-lasting. In addition, we have seen a number of smaller changes taking place, such as nationalist rhetoric turning dogmatism into a national character trait, open-mindedness taking the place of *Kritik* as dogmatism's most important other, social scientists developing quantitative methods for diagnosing closed-mindedness, philosophers of science challenging the term's pejorative connotations, and old formulaic expressions like "scientific dogmatism" being replaced by modern ones like "the two dogmas of . . ." and "challenging the dogma of . . ."

In addition to these changes over time, we have seen examples of meanings co-existing alongside each other, sometimes to the confusion or irritation of the scholars involved. A case in point is the explanation that Auguste Comte's British translator had to add to *A Discourse on the Positive Spirit*: Comte's understanding of dogmatic reasoning as the crown of scientific achievement was diametrically opposed to William Whewell's more conventional view of dogmatism as a stumbling block to scientific progress. Likewise, Karl Popper's condemnation of Thomas Kuhn's musings on the role of "dogma" in science illustrates that the two philosophers understood the term in rather different ways. Such co-existence of meanings, we have suggested, was the rule rather than the exception. There was always debate on how dangerous, permissible, or unavoidable dogmatic thinking was—with different definitions translating into different risk assessments.

Amidst all this change and disagreement, however, we have found three layers of meaning that were both persistent and influential in the long run. Indeed, their dominance was such that they effectively defined the term for generations of nineteenth- and twentieth-century scholars. The oldest of these, with roots in the seventeenth century, was the idea of dogmatism amounting to a character trait detrimental to the pursuit of learning. If the adjective "dogmatic" originally referred to a systematic mode of organizing or presenting knowledge, "the vanity of dogmatizing" as criticized by Joseph Glanvill and other seventeenth-century men of learning turned the method into a vicious trait of character. Although the former meaning did not cease to exist, it was the latter that achieved a dominant status in the modern period. For most of the authors featured in this book, being a dogmatist amounted to suffering from a vice that badly affected one's suitability for scholarly work.

Equally influential were a second and a third layer of meaning, both of which were usually grafted on the first one. The first of these is the idea that dogmatism was out of joint with the modern, critical age. Following the example of Immanuel Kant, nineteenth-century scholars often depicted dogmatism as a vice obstructing the advance of learning by refusing to let go of old-fashioned, outdated, or archaic modes of thinking. To the extent that progress was framed as "modern," dogmatism was relegated to the past. In this scheme of things, dogmatism came to serve as the very other of scientific progress and hence as a negative identity marker for both individual scholars and the pursuit of science at large. Chapter 8 suggested that this layer of meaning outlived the age of progress that the nineteenth century was: the late twentieth- and early twenty-first-century habit of contrasting dogmatic thinking with scientific innovation basically followed the same argumentative pattern.

The third fundamental layer of meaning that this study has identified added a specific texture to this "temporal othering" by associating dogmatism with clerical authority. As shown in Chapter 4, both British and German contributors to the post-Darwinian controversies of the 1870s frequently compared their opponents to pope-like figures who stuck to their views as if they were religious creeds. Interestingly, it was not only Darwinian biologists who accused their Christian critics of such dogmatic habits but also the other way around. Especially in the popular press, "the Haeckels, the Spencers, and the Huxleys of the present day" acquired a reputation for thundering ex cathedra pronouncements on themes beyond the boundaries of science. Although these clerical connotations became less pronounced in the more recent past, due perhaps to the declining significance of the church as a cultural point of reference, we have argued that echoes of this line of reasoning can be discerned in the still common equation of dogmatism with believing on authority. Especially in the critical thinking movement and in the burgeoning fields of virtue ethics and virtue epistemology, dogmatism is still invoked as the negative counterpart of free, independent, critical thinking.

In identifying these three layers of meaning as more influential and long-lasting than others, we do not suggest that other meanings of the term were merely ephemeral. For instance, while dogmatism has predominantly been understood as a character vice, Chapters 2, 6, and 8 have shown that this was not always the case. It was only in the seventeenth century that dogmatism was turned into a vicious habit of mind. Older meanings of the term survived, most notably in the form of dogmatism as a systematic mode of ordering knowledge appropriate to student textbooks and university lectures. Moreover, due to scholars' growing reluctance to engage in ad hominem reasoning, the character vice that dogmatism was long understood to be gradually turned into a theory vice—a quality not of persons but of theories. Accordingly, the vice referred to in the subtitle of this book was never alone: it was preceded, accompanied, and partly replaced by other notions of dogmatism.

All of these observations are about the *meanings* of dogmatism—the historians' most conventional level of analysis. Throughout the book, however, we have analyzed the scholarly discourse on dogmatism at two more levels. We have also examined the *functions* of the term, especially in academic debates (why did scholars accuse each other of "dogmatism"?), and the use of *repertoires* (why did people hark back to older meanings and uses of the term?).

As for the functions that the term fulfilled, one of our most striking observations is that charges of dogmatism, especially if made in the heat of controversy, did more than identify a character flaw with detrimental effects on the quality of published research. Accusing a colleague of dogmatic thinking amounted to throwing doubt on the person's very aptitude for scholarly work. More specifically, it did so by implying that the person's qualities belonged to other segments of society—parliament, church, or the private sector—rather than to science. "Pope Huxley," for instance, was a phrase implying that Thomas Huxley's uncompromising advocacy of evolution theory was more reminiscent of an episcopate defending its doctrines than of humble scientific inquiry. Likewise, because of its susceptibility to ideological manipulation, the dogmatic personality as defined in Cold War America was perceived as foreign to an academic world that prided itself in its "democratic," anti-ideological commitments. Charges of "dogmatism" thus evoked the specter of scientific border transgressions—which may help explain why the term was often invoked at moments when the boundaries between science, religion, and politics were perceived as being at risk. To the extent, then, that dogmatism was depicted as a trait foreign to the scientific attitude, charges of dogmatism served as instruments in what Thomas Gieryn calls "boundary work": a policing of the border between science and non-science with the intent of declaring opponents personae non gratae.

This, in turn, allows for a second observation, namely that dogmatism, used as a polemical device in controversies over the demarcation of science and non-science, typically encompassed more than what philosophers call an epistemic vice. If the adjective "epistemic" refers to epistemic goals pursued by epistemic agents so that an epistemic vice is a habit of mind detrimental to the pursuit of knowledge, then the range of adjectives that can be applied to the vice of dogmatism as invoked by scholars in the nineteenth and twentieth centuries also includes "political" and "religious." For many of the authors featured in this book, dogmatism was dangerous to the extent that it threatened Christian theology, Cold War democracy, or freedom of education. This is not to deny that on other occasions the epistemic consequences of dogmatic thinking far outweighed the vice's religious or political implications. The point, however, is that we cannot *exclusively* frame it as an epistemic problem—at least not as long as we treat dogmatism as an actors' category.[1] That is why the subtitle of this book uses the broader category of "scholarly vices," as an alternative broad enough to encompass various overlapping kinds of expectations that scholars accused of dogmatism were perceived not to meet.

Given the current state of scholarship, it is difficult to say how atypical dogmatism was in this regard. Was dogmatism a broader vice than prejudice or speculation? Were accusations of dogmatism more serious in their implications than charges of inaccuracy? Although further research will be needed for answering these questions, there are reasons to believe that dogmatism was not the only scholarly vice imbued with implications far beyond the level of individual competency. Historians have pointed out that the virtue of impartiality rose to prominence in seventeenth-century Europe

---

[1] Following Camille Creyghton et al., "Virtue Language in Historical Scholarship: The Cases of Georg Waitz, Gabriel Monod and Henri Pirenne," *History of European Ideas* 42, no. 7 (2016): 924–36, we interpret the adjective "epistemic" in a weak (non-exclusive) sense rather than in a strong (exclusive) manner.

largely because of the confessional and political struggles inaugurated by the Protestant Reformation. Both a lack of impartiality and an excess of it could be framed as a way of fueling these conflicts rather than mitigating them.[2] In the nineteenth century, likewise, speculation was perceived as opening the doors to philosophical modes of reasoning that were anathema to the empiricist ethos of fact-oriented fields like physics and history, just as hypercriticism was framed as an overdose of critical acumen that could have devastating consequences if applied to Scripture.[3] What these examples rather tentatively suggest is that "dogmatism" was not the only vice-term that allowed scholars to accuse each other of putting the integrity of the scientific enterprise at risk. A solid test of this hypothesis, however, would require more in-depth knowledge of the evolution of virtue- and vice-terms, as well as studies examining their interplay in actual controversies—not only in the European and American settings to which this book has limited itself but preferably also in other parts of the world.[4]

Finally, there are the repertoires on which scholars drew in warning against the ills of dogmatism or in pointing out its legitimate place in scientific practice. Both of these lines of reasoning had roots in the early modern period. In framing dogmatism as a scholarly vice, nineteenth- and twentieth-century scholars followed in the footsteps of natural philosophers in seventeenth-century England. The idea of dogmatism hindering the progress of learning went back to Kant, whereas grand narratives of modern science trumping old-fashioned dogmatism followed the storyline of William Whewell's influential history of science. The argument that some degree of dogmatism is unavoidable, or even desirable, either in didactic settings or under conditions of "normal science" harked back to early modern notions of *medicina dogmatica* and *theologia dogmatica*, which in turn were indebted to Quintilian's distinction between dogmatic and elenctic modes of reasoning. When nineteenth-century scientists accused the church of fostering dogmatic instead of scientific thinking habits, they echoed eighteenth-century anti-clericalists like Voltaire. Twentieth-century psychologists associating dogmatism with premature closure were on the same track as Isaac Watts more than two

---

[2] Joseph H. Preston, "English Ecclesiastical Historians and the Problem of Bias, 1559–1742," *Journal of the History of Ideas* 32, no. 2 (1971): 203–20; Kathryn Murphy and Anita Traninger, "Introduction: Instances of Impartiality," in Kathryn Murphy and Anita Traninger (eds.), *The Emergence of Impartiality* (Leiden: Brill, 2014), 1–29, at 11–13.

[3] Sjang ten Hagen and Herman Paul, "The Icarus Flight of Speculation: Philosophers' Vices as Perceived by Nineteenth-Century Historians and Physicists," *Metaphilosophy* 54, nos. 2–3 (2023): 280–94; Herman Paul, "Hypercriticism: A Case Study in the Rhetoric of Vice" (submitted).

[4] The research project "Scholarly Vices: A Longue Durée History," from which this study of dogmatism emerges, will make some further contributions to this effort.

centuries earlier ("the *Dogmatist* is in haste to believe something; he can't keep himself long enough in Suspence"). Or to mention yet another example: phrases like "challenging dogma with data" as used in scientific article titles are reminiscent of nineteenth-century worries about believing on authority—perhaps even of Hobbes' view, back in the seventeenth century, that dogmatists relied on "the authority of men" or custom. What these examples show is that modern scholars, consciously or not, stood in a long tradition of thinking about dogmatism—a discursive tradition full of allusions, echoes, cross-references, commonplaces, and other forms of intertextuality.

Admittedly, the degree of intentionality with which modern participants echoed or even relied on earlier voices in the tradition is not always evident. It is unknown, for instance, to what extent Wayne Booth was familiar with nineteenth-century critiques of "scientific dogmatism," or whether Kuhn had ever heard of "dogmatic chemistry" as laid out in student textbooks. By contrast, the reuse of older formulae often seems deliberate in the case of bon mots and quasi-proverbial phrases like Kant's "dogmatic slumber," W. V. Quine's "two dogmas," and the stock phrase "challenging the dogma of . . ." Appealing to the wisdom of the past was a way of invoking past authorities. It amounted to saying: "You are guilty of a vice that has been recognized long ago as detrimental to true scholarly work." What this appeal to the past added to charges of dogmatism was, accordingly, the weight of tradition. It justified the accusation by anchoring it in a centuries-long history of thinking about dogmatism.

This in turn brings out the benefit of studying scholarly vice language with the methods employed in this book. If there is anything that our analysis along three axes reveals, it is how heavily the shadow of the past looms over modern discussions of "dogmatism." Even if scholars sometimes seem unaware of the history of the term, its meanings and connotations as well as its effectiveness as a polemical device can be understood only against the historical background that this book has sketched. The continuity-in-discontinuity that we have mapped should, consequently, be understood in historical terms—not as a universality transcending the vicissitudes of history or as an endless process of change but as the emergence of certain patterns of thinking, reasoning, and polemicizing that, for shorter or longer periods of time, managed to define the parameters within which the term could be meaningfully used. The three overlapping key elements of our story—dogmatism as a character vice, a relic from the past, and a mode of believing on authority—were parts of a discursive tradition sustained by authors who invoked, repeated, applied, and modified them in new contexts. Dogmatism survived the passage of time because it was recognized by generations of scholars as a powerful idiom for discussing perceived threats to cherished notions of scientific progress and free, independent, critical thinking.

Index